WON'T
SOMEBODY COME
CORRECT?

DR. JACQUELINE
LAWRENCE

WON'T
SOMEBODY COME
CORRECT?

WON'T SOMEBODY COME CORRECT?

A New Spirit Novel

ISBN-13: 978-1-58314-464-0
ISBN-10:   1-58314-464-1

This publication contains the opinions and ideas of its author. It is intended
to provide helpful and informative material on the subject matter covered.
It is sold with the understanding that the publisher is not engaged in rendering
psychological, medical or other professional services. If expert assistance or
counseling is needed, the services of a competent professional should be sought.

® and TM are trademarks. Trademarks indicated with ® are registered in the
United States Patent and Trademark Office, the Canadian Trade Marks Office
and/or other countries.

www.kimanipress.com

Printed in U.S.A.

Special Thanks To:

- My earthly father, a big and bold man of God, affectionately known as "Bubba," from whom I inherited my impatience in dealing with the shortcomings of people, but nonetheless, who set a good example of the way we should treat one another, by treating others the way he wanted to be treated, and by utilizing every opportunity he had to teach others to do the same.

- My sweet, dear and loving mother, from whom I inherited my people-pleasing nature, but nonetheless taught me patience, unconditional love and understanding of the inadequacies of others.

- My Lord and Savior, Jesus Christ, who has kept me encouraged during my many challenges in dealing with people as He, through His Holy Spirit, inspired the writing of this book. I further thank Him for my beautiful parents and for teaching me to live and to love like Him through His Word by helping me to overcome my people-pleasing nature (like my mom) and my impatience in dealing with people (like my dad), thus bringing me to a place of loving my brothers and sisters unconditionally and with patience and understanding (like my mom) and by treating them the way that I want to be treated as I teach others to do the same (like my dad).

Table of Contents

"Because by one sacrifice he has made perfect forever
those who are being made holy."

(Hebrews 10:14)

"You were taught, with regard to your former way of life,
to put off your old self, which is being corrupted by its
deceitful desires; to be made new in the attitude of your
minds; and to put on the new self, created to be like
God in true righteousness and holiness."

(Ephesians 4:22–24)

"The tongue has the power of life and death,
and those who love it will eat its fruit."

(Proverbs 18:21)

"Beware of your friends; do not trust your brothers. For
every brother is a deceiver, and every friend is a slanderer.
Friend deceives friend, and no one speaks the truth."

(Jeremiah 9:4–5)

"Then He said to His disciples, 'The harvest is
plentiful but the workers are few.'"

(Matthew 9:37)

"And He is the head of the body, the church."

(Colossians 1:18)

Trying To Walk Correct

Because by one sacrifice He has made perfect forever those who are being made holy. (Heb 10:14)

People...people...people! Man, oh man! Did the Lord ever make me live this book! Have you ever said or thought phrases like, "People make me sick," "People aren't right," "I can't stand people," "People are trifling, a trip, awful," or worse? Have you ever asked yourself, "What's wrong with people?" Do you ever get tired of dealing with people because every time you do, somehow you always get the raw end of the deal, being inconvenienced by the inadequacies of everyone else? Do you ever feel like going somewhere so you can be alone and hide out and not have to deal with anyone; your friends, family, church members, people on the job? Do you ever wonder if you will have to succumb to a life of loneliness in order for you not to continue getting hurt by people? Do you put your trust in people over and over again, only to be taken advantage of time and time again? Have you ever gotten so sick and tired of being hurt, abused and misused that you made a vow never to help or to love anyone ever again? Well then, it's good to know that I am not alone. (You know what they say... "Misery loves company.")

God purposely allowed me to go through struggle after struggle, person after person, frustration after frustration, and test after test so that I would be able to deliver His God-given revelations in my struggle to love His people in spite of their many imperfections. With such a title, *Won't Somebody Come Correct?,* you can best believe that the fruit of the Spirit (love, joy, peace, patience, kindness, goodness, faithfulness, gentleness and self-control—Gal 5:22) has been greatly tested in my heart over and over again. As a result, I am fully convinced that the Lord has allowed me to be put in, to have gone through, and to be brought out of so many trials and tribulations in my dealings with people—not only for His sake and for mine, but also, for your sake, in hopes that you may learn some of the same valuable lessons of endurance, through the testing of my faith.

I further believe that I have been faced with so many challenges because I asked the Lord to use me to help to train up His people, making disciples of them. Through it all, however, my faith has been strengthened, and I have learned to faithfully love my brother, and am grateful for the opportunity to have endured my hardships and to share some of my struggles with you, in hopes that all mankind can come to a place of appreciating their own hardships, and to a place of loving each other; treating each other the way we all want to be treated—with unconditional love.

In writing this book, I have come to understand that when Christ is in us, He can be seen through us. However, oftentimes (even with people who profess to be in Christ) we have selfish ambitions, cannot be trusted and are inconsiderate of others. Being one who professes Christ Jesus as my Lord and Savior, as embarrassed as I am to admit it, because of these negative qualities that most people possess, I, too, have experienced great difficulty in trying to love them. Truthfully speaking, because of my frustrations in dealing with the ways people have treated me, not coming correct, there have been times when I have thought, "How can I get away from all this? Where can I run? Where can I hide?" I have also fantasized about resting in the bosom of Jesus or being caught up in the air to meet Him in the rapture just so I could get away from it all.

Sometimes...I Ain't Gonna Lie

Sometimes...I ain't gonna lie;
I can't stand some 'a y'all,
simply because you act like you can't stand each
other.
Look at the way you treat one another.
You act like you're afraid of guns, wars and bombs,
but the folk of whom you need to be scared is
each other.
Everyone seems to be all about what they can get.
They don't care whose heart they step on to get it.
Everybody's tryin' to come out on top.
You don't stop
to think about how the things you do
make others feel.
Won't somebody come correct?
Won't somebody keep it real?
Won't somebody out there love
by putting aside the way they feel?
Won't somebody desire to hear the truth,
no matter who the beneficiary?
Doesn't anyone want to hear good news
about someone besides "I, myself and me"?
Won't someone be first to love—
someone be first to give a hug,
someone be the first one to forgive;

to help folk with the lives they live?
We place no value on the lives of human beings.
Our loyalty goes out to status and things.
Will we ever learn?
We've been given chance after chance.
We deserve what we get, as far as I'm concerned.
Look back over our history.
God's been more than patient with us.
Will we ever get enough?
I don't know, y'all...
Sometimes...I ain't gonna lie.

When I began to focus my thoughts on how much God loved us (in spite of our many shortcomings) as evident by Him sending His Son to this earth to die for us all, and how much His Son, Jesus Christ, loved us, as evident by His suffering and dying for us, then I began to understand the true meaning of love. When I present the question *"Won't Somebody Come Correct?"* what I am asking is, "Won't somebody strive to live like Jesus; to do what Jesus would do, so that the glory of God can be seen in us through Jesus Christ who lives in us, as evident by us doing His will and that which is pleasing to Him through Christ Jesus?

Although Christ endured persecution after persecution for our sake, He made the choice to love us enough to give up His life for us. As He was dying on the cross, one of the last statements He made to His

Father was, "Father, forgive them, for they know not what they are doing." (Lk 23:34) I came to understand that if people did not know what they were doing to Jesus Christ as important and powerful as He was—rejecting and mistreating Him—in spite of all He did for them, then they certainly are not going to know what they do to me, and thus, loving and forgiving them, in spite of their ignorance, became easier for me. I further began to realize that it wasn't me who they were rejecting, but the Christ in me, and that they reject the Christ in me because they do not know the One who sent Him (Jn 15:21).

It's Not Me

It's not me who man rejects,
but the Spirit of God, in me,
who they reject as their king.
As I look at the life of Jesus;
one who was despised by men,
a man of sorrows and sufferings,
the Living Stone,
who has become the Capstone—
the Stone that the builders rejected,
but was chosen by God,
and precious to Him—
I, too, like living stones,
am being built into a spiritual house
to be a holy priesthood,
offering spiritual sacrifices;
acceptable to God through Jesus Christ.

The Israelites rejected His covenant,
broke down His altars,
and put His prophets to death with the sword.
They rejected His decrees and the covenant
He had made with their fathers
and the warnings He had given them.
They spurned the Word of the "Holy One of Israel."

Like one from whom men hide their faces.
He was despised,
and we esteemed Him not.
The wise have rejected the Word of the Lord.
What kind of wisdom do they have, then?
For if their rejection is the reconciliation of the
world,
what will their acceptance be,
but life from their dead?

I thank God for rejection!
For when I realized that people
were rejecting the Christ in me;
His goodness and His righteousness,
I thanked the Lord.
After looking at the type of people
who had rejected me,
believe you me, I thanked Him.
When I saw that they were not good
for me to have in my life
for one reason and another, anyway,
I thanked the Lord.
When people started to disappear from my life
without so much as a reason why,
I thanked Him.
When friends stopped talking to me
because of their outstanding balances with me,
I thanked the Lord.

When people started telling me no,
I knew that it was time for me to go,
and I thanked Him.
When the Spirit goes out in front of me,
joining me only with those who truly love me,
I thank the Lord.
When He does the accepting for me
and all of the rejecting for me,
I thank Him.
Praise be to God,
who has not rejected my prayer
or withheld His love from me!

Admittedly, the primary goal for my life is birthed out
of a somewhat selfish ambition; to live eternally in a
beautiful mansion that Jesus is preparing—or has already prepared—for me (Jn 14:2 KJV). I am not, however, trying to stomp on everyone else to beat down
heaven's door in order for me to get there, for I know
that it awaits me, and in God's time, I'll get there. Instead, I am trying to gather up an army of people who
are willing to fight life's battles in the Spirit as we enter
heaven's gates together, declaring that Jesus Christ is
King of Kings, and Lord of Lords. Because I place my
focus on storing up riches in heaven, I am under spiritual obligation to love everyone and treat everyone
right.

I know that in spite of the way people treat me, it is necessary for me to live my life in a way that is pleasing to God; walking blamelessly, doing what is right, speaking the truth from my heart, not having slander on my tongue, doing my neighbor no wrong, casting no slur on my fellow man, despising vile men but honoring those who fear the Lord, keeping my word even when it hurts, lending my money without charging excessive interest rates and not accepting bribes against the innocent. All of these areas deal with me loving my fellow man, coming correct and treating everyone kindly. As much as I sometimes may not want to love, come correct and be kind, but instead, may want to hate people who do me wrong, seek out vengeful ways to hurt them back and gloat over their failures, I know that this is not godly thinking, and that I must change my way of thinking to one that would be pleasing to God. I know that, as a Child of God, I must always treat people right; being truthful, building them up, respecting them, keeping my word and being fair. If I do not treat people right, then I can't love them, and thus, can't love God, which means that there will be no mansion for me in His kingdom.

This Is Why

One day, I approached the Lord and asked Him,
"Why do these things always happen to me?
I go through so much persecution,
that others even agree
that for some reason, I am often a target
for the enemy's attacks."
He showed me a glimpse of heaven
and a beautiful, crimson velvet curtain was
pulled back.
The most beautiful mansion
that human eyes couldn't bear to see
was standing there, glimmering with splendor,
almost blinding me.
As He handed me a set of keys,
with a bright smile, He replied,
"Take these keys to the place, my child,
as this is the reason why."

Now, as much as I try to come correct, I am in no way claiming to always be right and without fault, as I stumble in many ways, but I do aim for perfection because the Lord told me to be perfect (Mt 5:48). Because I have been cleansed by the blood of Christ who has taken away my sins, and because I press toward the goal of being perfect by striving to live like Jesus

Christ, I am being made holy by Him, as evident by me loving my brothers—even my enemies. I believe that if it were not possible for me to be perfect, God would not have commanded that I be so, and therefore, because with God all things are possible, it is He who is doing a perfecting work in me through His Son, Jesus Christ.

Perfection is not determined by man's standards—outward beauty and always being right and without fault—but by God's standards: complete in various applications of labor, growth, mental and moral character, etc.[1], with the understanding that there will be good times and bad times, and since God has made them both, we cannot discover anything about our future, and that all things work together for the good of us who love the Lord and those of us who are called according to His purpose.

Jesus said to a rich man in Matthew 19:21, that if he wants to be perfect, he must go, sell his possessions and give to the poor, and he will have treasure in heaven. Then come and follow Him. In order for a man to give up all that he has and to follow God, he must reach a certain level of spiritual maturity. God wants us to give to Him and to others that which we

[1]Strong, James S.T.D., L.L.D. *Strong's Exhaustive Concordance of The Bible with Dictionaries of The Hebrew and Greek Words of the Original with References to the English Words.* (Christian Heritage Publishing Company, Inc., 1988), p.71, 5046.

idolize and put before Him, so that He will be first in our lives. He is jealous and desires that we would seek first His kingdom and His righteousness. In our seeking, if we seek Him with our whole heart, then we will find Him. Oftentimes, we spend our time seeking after things—money, nice cars, homes and furniture—so people can form high opinions of us, a mate, friends, or we aggressively pursue career development. But some of us want time to ourselves so we can "veg out" and be lazy, not caring what others think.

There was a time in my life that I yearned for constructive criticism from others, in an effort to make myself perfect. However, I was trying to obtain perfection through the eyes of man, and not God. I began to realize that people's perceptions of how I should be were usually based on how *they* were, how they *thought* they were, or how they *sought* to be. For example, most of the women whose opinion of me I recruited said that I was too bold. For me, this was a compliment because they were not aware of all of the insecurities that I had to get past in order to get to be bold. After I explained to them where I came from, and how I struggled to get to where I was, they usually admitted that they wished they were more that way. Men oftentimes perceive me as being too intimidating. When I think about how weak some of them are, I am able to understand why they would think that.

It wasn't long before I stopped recruiting people's ever-changing opinions of me and how I should be, and began to look at the life of Jesus Christ as the standard for how I should be; accepting, bold, forgiving, humble, righteous and loving.

At one time, I assumed that the goal of every Christian man and woman was to be presented perfect in Christ, but I came to realize that everyone who proclaims to be a Christian is not a true Christian, thus everyone does not have perfection as his goal. When this realization hit, I began to experience a major turnaround in my life because I stopped expecting perfection from others, but instead, began to arm myself for their imperfections, and focus on my own. I came to learn that I could not change the heart of any man—not even my own—as only God can do that. Thus, through the inspiration of the Holy Spirit, I began to work on myself to become more noble, kind, loving, gentle and peaceful, so that I could be pleasing to God, while at the same time, allowing my light to shine before men so they could see my good deeds and begin to praise my Father in heaven.

Gratefully accepting my position as a disciple of Christ Jesus, it is my responsibility—as it is the responsibility of all Believers—to teach others to obey all of His commands. Like most of you, dealing with people, and trying to teach them, is oftentimes difficult, disappointing and frustrating because it seems as though most people do not want to come correct. The ones who do want to come correct, I've discovered, have two things in common: they strive to always keep their conscience clear before God and man, and they have a willing spirit. These are the people who are willing to offer the Lord their money, their work, their praise and their lives. They are willing to serve God by lending Him their ears and their minds, by lightening the load of others, giving, testifying, associating with people of low position, letting go of their possessions, sharing and serving others.

Even though it may be difficult to teach people to love one another and to come correct, if we, ourselves, truly love God and our brothers and sisters, then we will teach them all, because Jesus, who loved us all enough to die for *all* of us, commanded that we do so (Mt 28:20). As we teach others, I've discovered, in the process, we will become stronger men and women of God because we are also being taught by Him. The Bible tells us to apply our heart to understanding (Prv 2:2). It further tells us to train a child in the way he should go, and when he is old he will not turn from it (Prv 22:6). I had to come to an understanding that many of us were not trained correctly, and therefore, similarly to what Jesus said, they do not know how to come correct. We who have an understanding must teach those who do not, and help to train up God's children. In training them up to be mature, we must train them to be dependent on God, just as we, ourselves, are being trained by Him by constant use of distinguishing good from evil. Therefore, in training them, we must not be codependent, allowing them to lean on us, but encouraging them to lean on God and trust in Him, as we are learning to do.

I, like many of you, have been frustrated, angered, awestruck and saddened by the ungodly attitudes of people with whom I have been acquainted in every area of my dealings; in businesses, in my family and friendships, in people of my own race as well as in people of other races, and even in the church. This book was not written to condemn man for our many shortcomings, for who am I but one who also falls short? Jesus Christ, Himself—He who was without sin—being much more qualified than I to condemn us all, did not even come to condemn us. However, truth be told, I have personally witnessed and experienced enough mistreatment to understand God if He wanted to condemn us all straight to hell. Thanks be to Him, however, for looking beyond our faults and seeing our needs.

It is not my intention to simply share my frustrations with you in order that I may vent my anger or gain sympathy from you for the hardships that I have endured in my dealings with people, as I, myself, have let go of each and every one of them. However, my intentions are to share with you some of the struggles that I have endured, in hopes that your hearts may convict you to come correct as you begin to recognize some of the ungodly ways that you, yourselves, might have treated people, and some of the ungodly thoughts that you might have had toward them because of the ungodly ways that you, too, were treated. In addition to sharing my struggles in my plight of perfection, I also share with you the godly ways that the Lord has helped me to get past them, in hopes that you, who are undergoing the same kind of sufferings, can identify with them through some of your own experiences so that you, too, might be strengthened, refreshed and renewed.

As a Child of God, I know that I must suffer for Christ's sake, as Christ suffered for me, and that through my suffering will come perseverance and strength.

Therefore, as I move on from persecution after persecution, I ask the Lord to help me to forget what is behind as I strain toward what is ahead: everlasting glory. For I know that my present sufferings do not compare with the glory that God will reveal in me. Therefore, I am learning to rejoice in my sufferings and have become thankful for the opportunity to share in them with Christ in order that I will be like Him in death. I am also learning to focus my thoughts, not on my sufferings, but on the noble, right, pure, lovely, admirable, excellent and praiseworthy things that came as a result of my sufferings, in order that the fruit of the Spirit might reign supreme in my life. Additionally, I am learning to appreciate the good and the bad times, and to appreciate the good in both of them.

Inasmuch as I have been frustrated, angered and saddened by people's unrighteous acts, every now and then, someone finally and actually does come correct, and my heart is gladdened, joyful and awestruck. The irony, however, is that after praising and thanking them for their good deeds and asking them if they have accepted Jesus as their Lord and Savior, many have not. A former landlord of mine happened to be one of those people. In sharing the salvation of Christ with him, I told him that his heart was cleaner than the hearts of many Christians that I know, and that because of it, God would be happy to have him as His Child, but that having a clean heart cannot save your soul. Years later, this man, whose heart was pure, called me, telling me that he and his wife had joined a church, accepted Jesus as their Lord and Savior, and were now Christians. Glory to God!

It's Your Attitude

You were taught, with regard to your former way of life, to put off your old self, which is being corrupted by its deceitful desires; to be made new in the attitude of your minds; and to put on the new self, created to be like God in true righteousness and holiness. (Eph 4:22–24)

In order for us to please God, we must change the attitude of our minds by putting away our evil desires of sin so that we will not be trapped by them like those who live according to the sinful nature, having their minds controlled by sin. In putting away our evil desires, not giving in to the lusts of our flesh, we must also put to death sexual immorality, impurity and greed. If, however, we fail to put off our old self, our mind and consciences will remain corrupted and hence, so will our actions.

In order for us to change our old attitude, we must be made new. If we are in Christ, through whom God reconciled the world to Himself, then God makes us a new creation so that we are created like Him in true righteousness and holiness. In giving us a new self, through a new birth, we are given—if we would receive it—a new and undivided heart and a new spirit of obedience. Our hearts of stone will be removed and we will be given a heart of flesh so that we can love as God loves. When we put away our evil desires and are given a new heart and a new spirit of obedience, we are given a new song to sing, a new name to be called, a new tongue with which to speak and a new life to live.

As brothers and sisters of Christ, true righteousness and holiness doesn't just happen to us or for us, but we have to be taught by the Spirit to be righteous and to live holy. In order for us to be taught, however, we must first lend our ears to teaching. For we know that faith comes from hearing the message through the word of Christ (Rom 10:17). As we hear more and more of the message of righteousness and holiness, those of us who are called to belong to Jesus Christ are called to the obedience that comes from faith. As we become more obedient, not giving in to our deceitful desires, we receive the benefit of living in peace, quietness and confidence; not because we are righteous and holy, but because we are being obedient and are being led to righteousness.

Inasmuch as we are all given an opportunity and are empowered to live upright, godly lives, satan does everything he can to try to stop us from doing so. He wants us to live defeated, ungodly lives—to be devoured by our worldly passions and hardships. God, on the other hand, wants us to live godly lives—in spite of our hardships—and have an attitude of victory, and not defeat. I've heard it said time and time again that since we all go through hardships, it's not what happens to you but how you handle it that matters. An older woman, affectionately known as Ms. Rose, a surrogate mother to my mom (now deceased), once summarized it for me by telling me, "It's your attitude, baby." From that point on, I stopped focusing my thoughts on my hardships—as I have found this to be unproductive—but more so on seeking out productive solutions for them.

I recently called an elderly friend of mine who lived in the deep country part of Alabama. The last time I spoke with her prior to this telephone call, she had been experiencing so many physical ailments that I really wasn't sure if she was still alive. With a chipper and youthful voice, to my surprise she answered her telephone and shared with me how she was doing. She told me how happy she was to have moved from the country, and into senior apartments in the city where she lived closer to her children and neighbors who cared about her and checked in on her on a daily basis. She further shared with me how, because of her diabetes, one of her legs had been amputated, and how she went on an outing three times a week to a nearby dialysis center for treatment. She was ecstatic because her children, although busy with their own families, came to visit her on a regular basis. Her positive attitude really opened my eyes and helped me to appreciate my problems as well as all of the good things that come my way as a result of them.

Because, even in the midst of adversity, I try to focus my attention on that which is true, noble, right and praiseworthy; I have no appreciation for people who constantly dwell on their problems. For some reason, it seems that the people who talk the most are people who either constantly brag about themselves, talk about all the things they are going to do and people who, with dreary voices, always harp on their problems and misfortunes. No matter what is going on in their lives, whether positive or negative, they always land their focus on the negative.

Some people can go on and on and on, trying to get you alone so they can trap you into some corner of a room. You try to interject an occasional "uh-huh" to act as though you're interested, but they cut you off before you can even get to the "huh." When you say you have to go, trying your best not to make up a lie as the reason you have to rush off so quickly, but hoping you'll just be respected for having to go, they crowd in even closer.

When I recall their previous major dilemma, where they also cornered me the last time I saw them, and am finally able get a word in edgewise to ask them how it turned out, I'm left wondering why they are still not harping on that problem, it is only then that I find out that God has already worked it out. So instead of talking about how good God is for working out their last major dilemma, they remain focused on the present one, putting aside the joy of their deliverance from the previous one. Even when I try to get them to look at God's goodness for bringing them out of their last problem and all the good that has come about as a result of it, they immediately redirect the conversation back to their present problems.

I believe that many people do not want solutions for their problems because even if they had solutions, they would just find new problems on which to focus. No matter how much they gain, they would rather focus on what they lack because they haven't given their life to the Lord; serving and following Him. Many would rather seek evil, as opposed to doing good, and thus, sacrifice their peace. Then, when terror comes, all of a sudden, they want peace, but they cannot find it.

Still, some people want solutions for their problems, but they want everyone else to provide them with the solutions. I have been acquainted with many people who have tried to drop their problems in my lap, expecting me to bear their problems, burdens and disputes all by myself. But how can I solve all of their difficult problems when I cannot solve even the smallest of my own? First, let me not be a hypocrite, and take the plank out of my own eye, so that I can see clearly enough to remove the speck from your eye.

Get It Off My Lap

Don't think I'm cold when I ask you,
"What are you going to do about that?"
That's just my way of letting you know
I don't want your problem in my lap.

My shoulders can't bear the weight of the world,
but I know of someone whose can.
Don't look to me for answers, when like me,
you have access to the Man.

Don't expect me to gain knowledge for you
when you won't even pray for yourself.
I don't carry a magic wand,
but came to know Him for myself.

The same power that God gave me,
you can get it too.
The only person who is stopping
you from receiving it is you.

You're supposed to seek first His kingdom
as I am learning to do,
but you look to everyone else for answers,
then expect to get a prayer through.

You'd better get your problems off my lap,
seek His face yourself and pray.
Don't trust that if you put it on me,
that that's where it won't stay.

Since God sends rain on the righteous and the un-righteous, I can guarantee that as you continue to live out your life, problems will, no doubt, come your way. The manner in which we handle these problems, how-ever, is what can make us or break us. Now, I just happen to have the answer to *every* one of our prob-lems—*every* calamity that we might face—and here it is: TRUST AND OBEY GOD! Most of us know this answer, and as easy as it is for us to give this com-mand to everyone else, for some reason, it is difficult for us to accept it for our own lives; our own issues and dilemmas.

We are so quick to say that we love God, but if we truly love Him, our desire would be to do His will and as we delight ourselves in Him, He will give us the desires of our hearts, then we will not continue to sin because He will take our sins away. There is a popu-lar saying that goes, "To know you is to love you." Many people only know *about* God, but do not know Him as their God, as Lord of their lives. Only those of us who know God can trust Him. Therefore, if we know and love Him, it is only then that we can trust and obey Him.

If we trust God, we will dwell in the land and enjoy safe pasture. Our righteousness will shine like the dawn, and the justice of our cause will shine like the noonday sun. If we trust in God, we will not be afraid, nor will we be shaken, but will endure forever. Sometimes, however, we put our trust in false gods; our own strength, our wealth, our careers, our own devices and deeds, man, rulers of the world, deceptive words, our friends and family, our beauty and our wickedness. When we put our trust in these idols, or false gods, we will be turned back in utter transparent shame.

When we obey God, we will eat the best from the land, a land that will abundantly flow with milk and honey. If we obey God, we will eat and be satisfied. We will be blessed and set high above the nations and we will be made prosperous. Sometimes, however, we choose to be disobedient and rebel against God through our sins, and thus become slaves to our sins, which leads to death, as opposed to obedience, which leads to righteousness.

When trials and tribulations come my way, I try to understand the reason that certain things happen to me. If I don't understand the reason, I pray to God for understanding, and He always shows me that many of my trials were self-inflicted and have either stemmed from my disobedience and/or lack of trust in Him. After praying for forgiveness for my disobe-

dience and/or lack of trust, and turning from my sinful ways, I then search my heart—where His word is
hidden—and gird up my weapons for the next time
that temptations come my way. Some challenges, I've
discovered, are not self-inflicted, but come about as
a testing of my faith to help me to persevere, and
thus, strengthen my testimony. Through all of my
trials, whether self-inflicted or not, I am learning to
be patient in my afflictions, and have come to the understanding that it was good for me to be afflicted so
that I might learn God's decrees. I therefore came to
trust in the Lord with all my heart and lean not on
my own understanding; in all my ways acknowledging Him, so that He would make my paths straight.

Many of the afflictions that have come my way
have been brought about by others. Loving people
who set out to do me wrong has been my greatest
challenge because my flesh wants to get them back
and do to them what they have done to me, if not
worse. Even though I withhold my vengeance, as the
Lord has told me to, still, admittedly, I have been
known, in the back—and sometimes even in the
front—of my mind, to entertain the thought of folk
getting paid back for doing me wrong, and the
thought alone of them being repaid has brought me
pleasure. I have even gone so far as to ask God, to
whom vengeance belongs, to at least allow me to see
His vengeance, so I will be at peace, knowing that

they, too, in some way, had to suffer, because of their wrongdoing to me. I admit, for example, to have driven past one of my enemy's homes in hopes of seeing her car broken down on the side of the road, after she damaged mine, and to hoping that another of my enemies has lost her job, after she quit working for me without giving me notice, and to wanting to be rude to someone who has been rude to me. Although not Christlike, there have been many times when the mere thought of getting folk back for the wrong they have done to me has brought me temporary peace. ❦

I'm 'A Get 'Chu Back

You got me; ah mo get 'chu back.
You did me; ah mo do you back.
You dissed me; ah mo dis you back.
You missed me; ah mo miss you back.
You hurt me; ah mo hurt you back.
When you least expect it, ah mo get 'chu back.
Don't go to sleep, 'cause ah mo get 'chu back.
Oh, I'll still be your friend to the end,
But until then, I gotta get 'chu back.
I won't be satisfied until I get 'chu back.

Inasmuch as I have wanted to do unto people the way people have done unto me, for fear that I might get got first, or do unto them worse than I thought they would do unto me, for fear that they might do me worse, my spirit reminds me that I am not to repay anyone evil for evil and that God will avenge and will repay and make my enemies a footstool for my feet. I am reminded that I am not to gloat when my enemy stumbles and falls or let my heart rejoice or it will lead to my punishment, nor am I to fret, but refrain from anger and wrath—as it only leads to evil. I therefore conclude that perhaps it is not such a good idea for me to always seek the Lord's vengeance; but to let go and let God and do what Jesus would do—love my enemies and pray for them, treat them good and bless them, trusting that God would devour those who devour me; plunder those who plunder me and despoil all who spoil me.

I further am learning to appreciate my sufferings that were caused by people—especially for my good deeds, because when I suffer for doing good—and endure it—this is commendable before God. 1 Peter 2: 20–24 reminds me that I was called to suffer because Christ suffered for me, leaving me an example to follow. "He committed no sin, and no deceit was found in His mouth." When they hurled their insults at Him, set a crown of thorns on His head, spit on Him, made Him carry the heavy cross and beat Him, He did not retaliate. When He suffered, because of His love for us, He made no threats. Inasmuch as God could get us all back for sinning against Him, and His Son, Jesus Christ, could have repaid us all evil for evil, insult for insult, and pain for pain, instead, we were given grace, mercy and peace, in truth, and in love.

Instead of getting us back, however, Jesus entrusted Himself to Him who judges justly, saying, "Father, forgive them, for they know not what they are doing." Although most of us are aware of our actions, we are not fully aware of the ramifications, magnitude or consequences of them. For example, people knew that they were hurling insults at Jesus, but they did not understand to whom it was that they were hurling their insults—the only begotten Son of the Most High King—God Himself, Savior and Lord of all who believe in Him. They knew that they were killing Him, but they did not understand who it was that they were killing—the Alpha and the Omega, the Beginning and the End. Similarly, I believe that most of the people who have caused me to suffer are aware of their actions, but they know not to whom they are causing the suffering—a Child of God, Heiress to His throne and joint Heir with His Son, my brother, Jesus Christ—nor are they aware of the consequences they will face for causing me to suffer. For those who plow evil and those who sow trouble, reap it. At the breath of God they are destroyed; at the blast of His anger they perish (Job 4:8–9).

I believe that, at times, people may think that I am weak when I allow them to treat me wrongfully. But sometimes, in bearing with their failings (Rom 15:1), I just sit back and watch people try to play with my intelligence as they waddle in their own ignorance, as it is *they* who do not understand what they are doing and to whom they are doing it. It is *they* who will reap evil and trouble for sowing it. And it is *they* who are weak for feeling strong just because they have caused another to suffer. All the while that they do this, they think that I am unaware of what they are doing, and that they are…

Playin' With My Intelligence

Did you think I didn't know what you were up to when
you took so long to go 'head and dig in
your purse, while waiting for me to jump in mine
because you were taking up so much time,
hoping I'd hurry and say, "I got it, girl,"
because of my unbridled benevolence?
You're playin' with my intelligence.

Did you think I didn't know,
just because it didn't show
that I knew you were telling me a lie
when you couldn't even look me in the eye—
the same eye over which you tried to pull the wool—
when you told me what took you so long to come home
and where all the money went?
I'd say, you're playin' with my intelligence.

Did you think that because I might wear pink,
that there's a space in my head, causing me not to think?
Don't you know that because I'm bigger than you,
there are many things you do, that I can see through?

Sometimes, I just get tired of rebuking folk,
and instead, laugh inside when I see them work-
ing with diligence
to try to play with me, and my intelligence.

Maybe you don't know that I can see through you,
but just because I don't call you out on all the
devious things you do,
doesn't mean I don't know, or care.
I'm just hoping that deep down inside that
you'll spare
me the agony of losing yet another so-called friend.
Sooner or later, though, I'll have to stop the pretense,
so you can stop playin' with my intelligence.

You couldn't understand why everyone else did
me wrong.
You even said that in my life, they did not belong.
But when I told you I was having some major
trust issues with you,
and that time and time again, I felt used and
abused,
I thought you would have sense enough to correct
your ways.
But, my telling you still didn't stop your negligence,
because you still continued to play with my intel-
ligence.

I don't need to keep proving your wrongdoings in
every situation.
My silence means I'm constantly making an
evaluation.
And when I feel that I've given out enough bene-
fit of doubt,
as much as I hate to—because I like you—I have
to pull out
of this draining relationship
so I will no longer have to experience
you playin' with my intelligence.

In playing with my intelligence, people sometimes conspire and plot evil against me. Like God, in whose image I am made, although I get angry with them, I know that their day is coming, and I am oftentimes humored by their wicked schemes, and sometimes I can't help but laugh at their ignorance. My imagination causes me to believe that once Jesus' work was finished here on earth and He was taken up into heaven to sit at the right hand of His Father, He propped up His feet on a big, fluffy ottoman, reclined His chair, stretched out His hands and clasped His fingers behind His head, and the two of them, He and His Father, although still angered by our wickedness, are watching us and cracking up at our ignorance, as if they were watching a comedy movie. People think they are so slick in their evil pursuits, assuming that no one knows what they're up to, but even when no man knows, God knows and sees everything, and will one day judge men's secrets through Jesus Christ.

When I hear people hinting to me about the things they want from me, waiting for me to jump in and rescue them because they lack the courage to come out and ask me for what they want, sometimes, I just laugh to myself. When I hear people stumbling over lie after lie because they are not secure enough within themselves to tell the truth, I laugh. When I hear people talking about others for doing the same things which they are guilty of doing, because they can see everyone else's faults but their own, I just laugh to myself. When I hear people brag about how they come from a family with lots of money but they themselves don't have anything of value, I laugh.

I've noticed that a major cause of people's wicked schemes stems from their own insecurities due to a lack of self-worth. Although low self-esteem is a state of mind, so is self-esteem that is overinflated. Oftentimes people's insecurities are camouflaged with the appearance of high self-worth (thinking high, and oftentimes, even more highly of oneself than they ought). They try to deceive everyone else into thinking that they are "all that," but instead, because they think that they are something, when, like the rest of us, without the love of God, they are nothing, they deceive themselves.

Although people boast and brag about their possessions, their physical appearance, the work of their hands, because we are *all nothing* without the love of God, not one of us has anything in our lives about which to brag but the goodness of God.

Even those of us who are Children of God cannot brag about being Children of God because it was not our choice to become Children of God, but God's Himself. We know we cannot brag about being righteous, because we understand that even our righteous acts are nothing but filthy rags, and that God is the only One who can declare us righteous through our obedience of His law.

Jesus Christ—He, who came to save the entire world, He, being the Son of God, and in fact, who, being in the very nature, was God—if anyone—could have considered Himself "all that"; but He did not. He could have boasted and bragged about all the people whom He healed and delivered, however, He admitted that He could do nothing by Himself but only that which He saw His Father doing. Instead of considering Himself to be "all that," He considered Himself to be nothing, and did not glorify Himself because He knew His glory meant nothing, and that the only thing that mattered was the glory that He received from His Father. If Jesus could admit to being "nothing" without His Father, I cannot understand how any of us could possibly think that we're... ✑

All That

You say you're all that, a bag of chips with dip.
You have a big booty, small waist and big hips.
You know how to work it in a tight knit dress,
but love is something that you don't possess.

You got your education with all your degrees;
your big, fine house and your grand benzies.
You send your children to the finest of schools,
but without forgiveness in your heart, you'll always lose.

You work out at the gym so you can keep fit,
parading around like you're the man who just
can't quit.
You brag about your six pack and all the weights
you lift;
got shallow-minded females thinking you're
God's gift.

You always receive, but you never give,
but God gave His Son so that you could live.
When people come to you with their burdens of
despair,
you change the subject to yourself as though you
just don't care.

You judge everybody because of their past mistakes,
but let them say one word about you, and see how
it makes
you go off—like you're too good to be discussed.
When judgment comes back, it never seems just.

You say you're all that, a bag of chips with dip,
so full of false pride and deceitful lips.
It's wonderful to feel good about oneself,
but not if you think you're better than everyone else.

If you want to be "all that" let me tell you how;
give up all your "all thats" for the Lord, right now.
Live, love and believe the way He wants you to.
Give to Him who is "all that" His due, through you.

Until these people who may think they're "all that"
submit themselves to the Lord, and not to the things
that they believe classify them as being "all that,"
they will never be satisfied. I've found that the ones
of us who are truly "all that" are not deemed as such
because of anything we do, because we know there is
no one who does good but God, and apart from Him,
we can do nothing. We who are truly "all that" don't
brag about being "all that" because we know that
what makes us "all that" is not who we are, but whose
we are. Because we know that God loves us, if we
boast, we boast in Him, and not ourselves, for it is He

who gives us the ability to produce our "all thats," our wealth, and brings us to a place of abundance. Although we may (or may not) be richly possessed with the things of this world, we know that the love of money is a root of all kinds of evil, so in order for our spirit to be blessed, it must remain poor so that we may inherit the kingdom of heaven.

Oftentimes, people boast about their wisdom, strength and riches and compare themselves with themselves, as though there is no standard higher than themselves. They expect everyone else to act the way they act, think the way they think, believe the things they believe and say the things they say, as though their way of doing things is the only "right" way. You might hear them saying things like, "I don't know why she did that, I would have never done anything like that to her." We should never be expected to pattern ourselves after any other person but Jesus Christ. ❧

I'm Not You

You have a law book of your very own
about the way everyone should be.
Your book dictates how we should all act,
as though you control our destiny.
You base the things that we should do,
on the things that you think you would do.
The problem is, you don't get to dictate
the walk that we take in our shoes.

I hope you don't take any offense to this,
but, with all due respect,
I wouldn't want to walk in your shoes
and take on your severe defects.
There are many issues in my own life
that I'm trying to clear up within myself,
so, unlike you, I don't have time to focus
my attention on everyone else.

Why judge my character based on the things
that you think that I should do?
I'll bet you anything that the biggest violator
of your own law book is you.
If you're not happy with what you see
from the eyes that you look through,
why expect me to live my life as though
my eyes are looking through you?

I'm not you, and you're not me.
Let's both be how we're supposed to be.
I'll respect you for the person who you are,
now you do the same for me.
Before you try to remove my specks,
make sure your planks are gone.
I am not you, and you are not the one
to whom I look up, or depend on.

Some people compare themselves with others who may not be as wise, strong or as rich as they are—even looking down on them as though such people are not even worthy of being in the midst of their company. Some people of non-color, for example, look down on people of color. Some slim people look down on heavy people, and some men look down on women—in order that their false pride might be boosted. Since I happen to be a heavyset woman of color, and am frequently looked down upon for being so, I am sure that I, too, can compare myself with others and find things in them whereby I can put them down in order to boost my own ego—but how would that benefit and enrich my life?

If I compare myself with those on whom I could look down because they lack certain qualities that I might possess, I might get high-minded, content with and prideful of the way that I am. If I compare myself with those who consider themselves to be more than me, then they, being imperfect, will always disappoint me. Therefore, instead of comparing myself to the least of them, or to those who consider themselves to be the most of them, I try to hang with the "People who try to live righteously," and thus, God is my measuring stick. When I compare myself with Him, even though nothing I do can compare with Him, then I am able to see my many shortcomings and strive to be more like Him—blameless, holy and perfect. Unlike man, God, who never lies, changes His mind, says He will do what He doesn't do, or makes promises that He will not fulfill, will never disappoint me.

Since we were all made by God through His Word and in His image to be like Him in true righteousness and holiness for His glory, and that everything He made is beautiful, wonderful and good, I am, therefore, in no position to look down on anyone—whether black or white, fat or thin, male or female. God knew what He was doing when He made us. Not one of us had any say-so about how He made us to be. He not only created our outer being, but He even created our inmost being (our emotions and moral sensitivity) in our mother's womb to do good works, which He prepared in advance for us to do. Because the Lord is firm in His purpose, which will always prevail, those of us who love Him and have been called according to His purpose know that we might as well just kick back and enjoy the ride because in all things, He works for the good. ♪

Destined To Be You

Way back when, before time began,
God had you in mind.
He made you special and unique;
to be one of a kind.
Only at that very instant could that one egg
have united with that one sperm,
to bring you into existence,
for your designated term.

Had that one egg
joined with any of the others,
you wouldn't be alive today;
you'd be your sister or your brother.
No matter how much like you,
they might be,
they could never, ever be
the "you" I see.

Only you can be you,
and no one else.
If there were no you,
you'd have no self.
God made you for His purpose
and His reasons.
He wanted to give you an opportunity
to be here for a season.

He gave you free will
to make your own choices.
Made you a book of people bold enough
to raise their voices
to show and tell you the way
that you should go;
even gave Himself as an example of how to love,
so you would know.

There is a path that is laid out
for me and for you.
Only you are meant to endure the things
that you go through.
When you make decisions based on
your God-given values and beliefs,
you begin to live out your purpose,
because being "you" gives you relief.

But when you dance to the beat
of other people's drum,
you're keeping a little of "you" for yourself,
and giving others some.
People who cannot accept, and who try to
stop you from being "you,"
are getting in the way of what
God wants to do through you.

How can you learn for yourself
to trust in the Lord

if all of your trust, in another,
has been stored?
God wants your heart
to be single and free
so He can design you to be
who He wants you to be.

Although God's design for each of our lives was
mapped out even before our very existence on this
earth, it is up to each of us to live our lives according to
His purpose, and He gives each of us a choice to do so.
Just like God has a purpose for each of our lives, however, satan, too, has a purpose of his own. Although
God's purpose for us is to have an abundant life, Satan's
purpose for each of us is death, lack and destruction. Everything God gives us, satan desires to take away. And
everything satan gives us, God desires to take away. It
is God's will that none of us will perish, but He left it
up to us to choose whom we will serve—Him or satan.
We must therefore obey God and seek Him and His purpose, for each of us has been uniquely designed by Him
according to His purpose for our lives, and was put here
to fulfill the destiny that He designed for our lives.

We were not all made to be alike, but all of our de-
signs are different—inwardly, as well as outwardly.
No two people look or act exactly alike—not even
identical twins. Folk tend to look down on, and iso-
late themselves from, people who are not like them—

people who do not think, believe, speak and behave the way they do, as well as those who are not of their same race, age or sex. People who are poor, needy and oppressed are often cast aside by higher achievers because they are looked upon as being in lowly positions. Instead of looking down on these folk who nobody else wants, and casting them aside, I try to lift them up to help them to get where I am trying to go, because I know that sometimes I am the only person they know who is willing to help them and not trample on them and do away with them. Helping these folk who nobody else wants around them, however, has been a challenge because inasmuch as I have tried to help them, I soon learned the reason why no one else is willing to help them: they have been burned over and over again by them. Oftentimes, while helping out such folk, I have found that the very mouths that I have fed are the ones that have turned around to bite me.

Because so many people have taken my kindness for weakness and because of the fact that I have been burned so many times by helping folk, it has become difficult for me to do so. Therefore, in order for me to protect my own best interest, I sometimes find it necessary to handle some of the folk, who nobody else wants, with a long-handled spoon. In my experience with dealing with these folk, I have concluded that many of them do not truly want a way out of their lowly positions, but only want someone around to whom they can complain about their problems and/or perhaps rescue them from their immediate situation. I have decided that I am not helping people if I am only giving them a temporary fix for their situation, especially those people who are hot-tempered, for they will only need to be rescued again, and thus, I stay away from these types of people and allow them to pay their own penalty.

As Christians, we are supposed to help our brothers and sisters who have physical needs, like food and clothing, if it is within our power to do so. Once their immediate needs have been addressed, then, if it is within our power, we should help them with their long-term needs—if our help is desired. When someone complains about being broke because they are unemployed, for example, I ask them about their job-seeking pursuits and oftentimes I find out that they have not put in any effort toward looking for a job. I found that it is better for both me and for them that I teach them how to fish, as opposed to my always giving them a fish. In this way, they are equipped to help themselves in the event that they find themselves in a similar situation in the future. Because I know that he to whom much is given, much is demanded, and to whom much is entrusted, much more will be asked, instead of pouring out major blessings and responsibilities upon them, I give them one small blessing or responsibility at a time to see if they will be faithful with the small things before I use my time, money and wheels putting the bigger blessings and responsibilities in front of them.

Perhaps I might start out by buying them a newspaper and helping them to seek out and circle job opportunities for which they might be qualified. If, after a few days, they have not even looked at the newspaper, let alone made any telephone calls to potential employers—especially after telling me they would—then, in being patient with them, I try to find out the reason they have failed to seek employment. If they are stuck in idleness, I warn them that an idle mind is the devil's playground, and if they remain idle, and are playing with the devil, I would have to leave them alone. If they are timid, I try to encourage them by letting them know that they can do everything through Christ, who gives us strength. If they are weak, I try my best to bear with their failings and give them further assistance by relieving them of some of their responsibilities—perhaps writing out a script for them to say to potential employers when they call them, or helping them to write a cover letter and résumé.

If I discover that someone does not want anything better for themselves, and are not willing to help themselves, but would rather remain poor (in spirit, wealth, health, etc.), then, I, too, am unwilling to help them. Before things get to a point where I am becoming poor as a result of my helping others—financially, emotionally, mentally, physically and spiritually—I most likely will withdraw my help, which was tossed aside anyway, but will continue to help them by praying for them to the One from whom our help comes.

God wants us to wholeheartedly seek Him first in everything we do; during the first second of the first minute of the first hour of the first day of the first week of the first month of the first year, at the very first moment when we are grateful, hopeful, blessed, fearful, struggling, desirous and troubled, before we seek out anything or anyone else—our mother's advice, a cigarette, the weather report, a doctor's opinion, our horoscope, a drink or a curse word. Unfortunately, however, in their seeking, many people, I've discovered, although they might go to God with questions, do not wait on Him for answers, and instead of seeking God, they go about seeking the things they want for themselves.

In helping people, I've come to learn that many people believe that they are entitled to receiving the things that I have just because they happen to know me, or perhaps, have done a favor for me in the past. They talk as though they don't believe that I deserve everything I have. They beg and wait around for the things that I no longer want as though I have to give these things to them. What they don't understand is that I've worked hard for everything that I possess.

Being a fairly successful business owner, at one time, I, a single parent who lived in a middle-class, culturally diverse neighborhood where both parents had to work outside of their homes in order to maintain their lifestyles, and to outsiders looking in, it appeared as though I had it made. What they did not see, however, were the large pile of bills I had to pay every month in order to keep everything I had, and how I had to work every day from the time my feet hit the floor every morning at sunrise, until the time my feet left the floor every night at bedtime. Nor did they hear all my cries and prayers for the Lord to deliver me from the stress of the many telephone calls that came from my creditors when I began to suffer financially.

I once had a home that was vacant for quite some time and many of my acquaintances started calling me to see if they could live there. On one occasion, the mom of one of my daughter's friends called me begging to let her and her children live in the house. Although I knew she couldn't afford to pay the amount of rent that the market would bear, I asked her for the amount that she could comfortably afford to pay me. Even though the amount that she said she could afford to pay was half of what I would have normally charged for rent, I allowed her and her children to live there, as she confided in me that her credit was bad and that it was difficult for her to find a place. She paid her rent the first month, on time. The second month, I had to beg her for it until, little by little, she paid it. Then, by the third month, I had to end up paying hundreds of dollars to have her evicted.

Because a friend of mine served her the eviction notice on my behalf, she went straight to the courthouse and had me served for harassing her regarding the rent payments. In total, she ended up living in my home for five months paying me for only two months' rent. Because I had to pay the equivalent of one month's rent for the eviction process, all in all, she ended up paying me for just one month to live in my home for a period of five months at a reduced rate—all because of my kindness.

Although this was a disheartening experience, my spirit of giving and kindness remained unbroken. Shortly thereafter, I met up with a teenage girl named Carol, who was the same age as my own daughter and who, at one time, was our neighbor. Her mother and father had abandoned her because she was rebellious and on drugs. She had nowhere to live but on the streets. I felt sorry for her, and because I had a house that was fully furnished yet temporarily unoccupied, I allowed her to live there for a few months so she could get a job and eventually a place of her own. The only stipulations I made were that she not do drugs in my home or have other people there. A neighbor who lived next to the house soon informed me that Carol had visitors over all hours of the night that were outside my home doing drugs with her. I paid her a couple of unexpected visits, and each time I went there, I found strangers passed out on my couches.

After listening to her lies and excuses a few times, I finally got fed up and told her she had to leave. She had the nerve to tell my daughter that the house was hers, that I couldn't throw her out, and that she was going to take me to court to make me go through an eviction process, in order for her to stay longer. I learned from my experience of renting my home to my first tenant, however, that if I did not charge rent, which I did not, then we did not have a tenant/land-lord arrangement, and that I could have her leave without having to go through the eviction process, so she was out of there immediately.

I later heard that Carol was prostituting and was now badly strung out on drugs. I went to the place where I heard she was living and prayed with her. She cried on my shoulder as I hugged her, told me how much my prayers and presence was a blessing to her, and how much she wanted to stop living the life she was living. I gave her some money so she could buy herself some food, along with my telephone number in the event that she would need me in the future. For a week straight, she called me every morning and left messages on my answering machine, telling me that she had no food. I could tell in her voice that each time she called me, she was high on drugs. Finally, I returned her calls and told her that I wouldn't give her any more money, but that I would gather together some food from my house and give it to her. She told me that she would call me back later that day to tell me when and where I could deliver the food. I didn't hear from her again until a few days later, when she called me, telling me she was hungry and asking for more money. I told her that I had gathered together some food for her a few days prior, as I told her I would, but she never called me back to let me know when and where I could deliver it. I also informed her that I knew she was high each and every time she called me, and that I knew she just wanted me to give her money for drugs. I then informed her that I would continue to offer her food if she needed it, and that I would keep her in my prayers.

On yet another occasion, a *good Christian friend* of mine was thrown out of her home. She had been living with her son, her younger sister, her mom and her sister's friend and baby. She asked me if she and her son could live in this same house, for one short month, until she could find another place. Our arrangement was for her to pay me for the utility bills that she and her son would incur while living in the home, but that she didn't have to worry about paying me any rent. Because she knew about all of the mess that I had previously endured with the others that I had allowed to move into my home, and because she was supposed to be my friend, I never expected her to take advantage of me like the others did.

I asked her who would be living there in the house. Her answer was, "Just me and my son." When I went to visit her, I found that not only were she and her son living there, but also her sister, mom, and sister's friend and baby. Playing ignorant when I confronted her about the lie she had told me, she said, "Oh, I thought I told you we were all coming." Sticking to my word to let her live there for a month, I let the lie slide.

Once the agreed-upon month was over, I waited for her to inform me of the day that she would be leaving but she said nothing. Seeing that she was dodging the many messages that I had left on her answering machine for her to let me know when she would be leaving, I decided to pay her a visit. Because she said that she had nowhere else to go, I agreed to let her stay at my home for two more weeks. When her two weeks were over, being the kind-hearted friend that I am, I helped her pack her belongings. Not only did she leave the state without paying me a dime for the utility bills that she and her family and friends had incurred, as promised, but she left her mom in my home because she had nowhere else to go, and I ended up having to force her out.

Inasmuch as I have tried to convince myself that

never again will I help out another person, my heart quickly rejects this idea. I know that if I am to come correct, I have to live as the Lord has told me to and look to Him as the icon for everything I do. Although my flesh wanted to hold grudges and harbor resentment and anger against these people who have done me wrong, in spite of how I helped them, I have had to ask the Lord to help me to forgive them and do good to them so that I may abound in love, as He always abounds in love for me; for I was once poor and in need, and He lifted me out of my affliction and increased my family like flocks. He opened His hand toward me, was not too proud to associate Himself with me, accepted me, and was gracious and full of compassion toward me.

At one time I, too, was foolish, disobedient, deceived and enslaved by all kinds of passions and pleasures. I, too, lived in malice and envy, being hated and hating my brother. But when the kindness and love of God appeared, He saved me—not because of righteous things I had done but because of His mercy. He saved me through the washing of rebirth and renewal by the Holy Spirit. I was nothing but filthy rags and He loved me. Therefore, as I continue to try my best to live with my brother in harmony, not withholding good from those who deserve it—the poor and needy—I, too, being made new in the atti-

tude of my mind to be like that of Christ Jesus, must
be sympathetic, loving, compassionate and humble
as my Father is toward me.

The Fruit of the Tongue

The tongue has the power of life and death, and those who love it will eat its fruit. (Prv 18:21)

It is important that we use our tongues wisely because what we say, and what we do not say, may cause either hurt and harm or healing and help to ourselves and others. If we speak wisely, then we will be full of wisdom. If we speak foolishness, then we will be full of foolishness. If we speak too much, we betray a confidence. If we speak too little, mercy may be withheld from us. Our tongues should be used to speak what is just, to sing, to tell of God's righteousness and to give faithful instruction. We should not, on the other hand, use our tongues to speak of deceit, evil, lies, flattery and wickedness.

As a Christian, I am compelled to treat my brother with goodness, regardless of the way I am treated; to love regardless of whether or not I am loved. In doing so, I must pay close attention to everything I say and do to my brother so as not to bring anyone harm, always being prayerful and acknowledging God in everything. When establishing any type of relationship, the need for open communication is crucial in order that the relationship might succeed. Parents say they want their children to come to them to talk to them about anything, bosses tell their employees to communicate with them regarding any problems they might be having on the job, boyfriends and girlfriends establish the necessity for communication in a relationship, and even God, Himself, wants us to pray to Him in the Spirit on all occasions with all kinds of prayers and requests. Communication has oftentimes been referred to as "the key" to making a relationship work.

The Key

Why does everyone always say
that communication is the key?
But when I tell folk about the way I feel,
they always get mad at me.
Folk can dish it out, but who can take
others telling them the truth?
All people want is to be pumped up
and to have their egos soothed.

It seems as though no one can handle
any kind of correction.
Nobody wants to change their ways
and head in a new direction.
They want me to walk on eggshells,
tiptoeing around their insecurities.
They feel more comfortable dealing with folk
who exist in mere obscurities.

Everyone wants a relationship,
but no one wants to relate.
Even when I try to talk nice to folk,
they swear I'm trying to mutilate
their character, just because I've lovingly
pointed out
one of their many flaws.

Folk are so quick to dismiss "friendships"
without having legitimate cause.

When I try to further explain my position,
they get loud and even more offended.
I thought I could at least keep it real
with folk in my life who I befriended.
I wish there was someone who could respect
the words that come from inside of me;
someone who really and truly believes
that communication is the key.

Inasmuch as I try to communicate openly, truthfully, respectfully and with wisdom, discernment and restraint, still, I have discovered that as long as my communication is agreeable with others and I am saying exactly what they want me to say and doing what they want me to do, I am considered to be "nice." But when I express my hurt, skepticism, mistrust, disappointment and anger about them, all of a sudden people get defensive and I become the "bad guy." When people do me wrong, somehow other people are able to understand how I feel. They even agree that I am right to feel the way that I feel. But when they themselves are the ones that I have to confront for doing the same thing to me, then all of a sudden I am the "bad guy" for even bringing my concerns to their attention. All of a sudden, the focus gets turned onto me for feeling the way that I feel, and I become every bad name in the book.

There used to be a time when it was important for me to be nice to people—giving in to their wants every time it was expected of me—in order that I might gain their approval. But then I realized that as long as I was trying to gain man's approval, I was not serving Christ because my aim should be to please Him, gaining His approval and not that of man's. When I started to focus my attention on gaining God's approval, then naturally I began to please man—not through the eyes of man necessarily, but through bearing with his shortcomings in order that I might build him up. Because I cannot possibly gain every man's approval of me, my focus has been shifted from being "nice" (giving to people's wants) to being "kind" (giving to people's needs).

In being kind, I learned that I benefit myself, because by focusing my attention on being kind, giving freely to those who deserve it—the poor and needy— I am honoring God, and thus will be rewarded and blessed. It is easy to give to people who are less fortunate than we are because they will most likely appreciate our kindness. The real challenge, however, is being kind to the wicked and the ungrateful. Although these people may not deserve our kindness, as we ourselves do not deserve our Father's kindness, still, God wants us to have mercy on them and to be kind, even to them, as He is kind and merciful toward all of us. When we are kind to the wicked and the ungrateful, not only will we be rewarded, but we will be *greatly* rewarded!

I had to come to realize that sometimes my being "nice" hurts and hinders others, as opposed to helping them, and in order for me to build them up, it may become necessary for me to not be "nice." Because God has a plan for all of our lives, sometimes even a plan for pain, in order for me to not interfere with that plan, it is sometimes necessary for me to withhold niceties in order that the plans of God might be fulfilled. There are lessons that God has for all of us to learn, but if I rescue people from all of their problems, then I am stunting their growth because they are not learning the valuable lessons that they need to learn for themselves. Sometimes, what people need is for you to just back off.

I don't have a problem with pleasing others, as long as pleasing them brings joy to my heart. But, although I do not *seek* to please myself, if pleasing folk means that stress, anxiety, feelings of being used, hurt, strife or any negativity will be added to my life due to my pleasing others, thus decreasing my own peace, then in such situations, it becomes necessary that I choose to please myself, because I cannot love others effectively unless I am first loving myself. Sometimes pleasing others may mean that I must withdraw from being nice to them in order that I might build them up by allowing them to see that they are not kind to themselves, me or anyone else, and they do not deserve to be pleased by me, but instead, they need to learn the lesson(s) they need to learn from God so that they may mature in Him.

Sometimes, when I tell people the things they *need* to hear, as opposed to that which they *want* to hear, or when I give people what they *need* rather than what they *want,* or when I take away from people that which *needs* to be taken away from them, they become offended and unyielding and I am no longer considered to be "nice," but all of a sudden I'm trippin' and I become the "bad guy."

Why I Got To Be the Bad Guy

Some folk may think
I'm a straight-up witch.
I've been called evil,
when I make the big switch
from being a warm person
who folk consider to be nice
to one who freezes up
and turns cold as ice.
Evil comes out of the devil,
who is nowhere in me.
I know my heart,
which only God can see.
My intentions are to never
cause anyone sorrow,
but to lead folk into
a brighter tomorrow.
As much as I love folk,
I love myself as much,
so sometimes I back off
to miss my enemy's touch.
I used to let folk walk over me;
back when I was young,
but now, when people do me wrong,
I don't always bite my tongue.
If folk expect me

to keep my big mouth shut,
don't start none, won't be none,
and I'll gladly shut up.
It's a trip to watch
how the tables get turned
every time I open my mouth
about my getting burned.
All of a sudden you've made me the bad guy
who has defiled you.
If I'm so bad, you could have opened
your mouth about me, too.
Why must you wait until I express my beef
before you tell me how you feel?
I shouldn't have to be the bad guy
just because I keep it real!

Instead of looking upon me as the "bad guy" just because I take advantage of an opportunity where I can help someone—to offer them an alternative way of thinking—why can't I be looked upon as a "good guy"? If I hold out on an opportunity to help someone who needs discipline or rebuke, then I am holding back on an opportunity to give them life. In helping people, it is my hope that as I offer my discipline through God's Word—as I am doing in this book—folk might use sound judgment and discernment, and make the necessary corrections in their lives, and would, thus, be given life.

All too often, when God does not come to our aid when and how we want Him to, or when bad things happen to us or those we love, we consider Him to be the bad guy. Instead of us putting our trust in Him, believing that all things are working together for our good, and that we are called according to His purpose, and not He for ours. We sometimes expect Him to serve us, as opposed to us serving Him; jumping to our every whim. Then, when He does not do what we want Him to do, we get mad at Him, thinking that He has done us wrong.

It's nice to be nice, but being nice is not always appropriate. I once observed two children who were fighting over toys. When one child had a toy that the other child wanted, she would complain to their mother about the other child not sharing. The mother would then tell the child who had the desired toy to "be nice" and to share. The children learned that if one of them was playing with a toy that the other wanted, she simply had to jerk it out of her sister's hands as she makes the demand to the other to "Be nice!" Because she has said these magic words, "Be nice," she automatically gets to keep the toy for herself, and the other child is left without the toy. Many children and adults think that they need to be nice to everyone, and thus, allow everyone to have their way with them. If children were raised to be kind, as opposed to "nice," in consideration of the other's feelings, one child might say to the other, "May I please play with the toy?" as opposed to, "Be nice," and then taking the toy. In being raised up to be kind, as opposed to being nice, they would be provided with the opportunity to learn some valuable lessons, which include:

- asking for what they want in a kindly manner, as opposed to demanding it
- considering other people's feelings, understanding that they may not want to comply
- realizing that they cannot always have their way
- dealing with rejection
- making choices as to whether or not they want to give
- being appreciative of the other person's choice to give, and thus being provided an opportunity to say, "Thank you"

At one time in my life, when people would call me nice, I was flattered, but when I realized that being nice meant pleasing everyone, telling them what they want to hear and doing what they want me to do, I began to let them know that my aim is not to be nice (pleasing in order to gain everyone's approval), but to be kind (doing good and being considerate of everyone). The Lord never told us to be nice to one another. As a matter of fact, when we go around trying to please everyone so that they will speak well of us, we are being fake, and are bringing grief upon ourselves.

Although God did not tell us to be nice, He did, however, tell us to be kind to everyone so that we can cheer one another up, honor Him, benefit ourselves, be blessed, renounce our wickedness and gain respect. God tells us that love is kind (1 Cor 13:4). Therefore, if we love one another in the way that He wants us to, we will be kind to one another; not pleasing everyone by doing and saying everything they want us to, and the way they want us to—in order to gain their approval—but by showing everyone goodness, compassion and consideration in how, what, when and where we say and do the things we do and say. ❀

There is, however, one particular area of my life where I find myself constantly trying to please folk; and this causes me to bite my tongue. I must be careful to utter wisdom and speak what is just, guard my lips as I guard my life, not to speak rashly so as not to come to ruin, for I know that the tongue has the power of life and death. There are so many things that I could say to folk to bring them down—especially after they try to make me feel bad—but because these things might be considered offensive, oftentimes I find that it is best that I silence my words, swallow my pride, humble myself and, for my own sake, as well as for the sake of others, I must sometimes be nice. People, I find, are not always ready to receive the things that enter my mind, so I know I must sometimes hold back from saying what is on my mind in order that they may not get angry, defensive, curse me out and end up hating me.

The Bible says that he who holds his tongue is wise (Prv 10:19) and that he who guards his lips, guards his life (Prv 13:3). Therefore, wisdom has taught me to use my words carefully, and not recklessly, lest they pierce like a sword. I know that I must allow the Holy Spirit to lead me in choosing my battles, so that I might bring healing and not harm to myself and to others.

What I've discovered, however, is that inasmuch as people say they want to hear the truth, and can handle hearing it, I can see in their faces—as evident by their eyes swelling with tears and fluttering with anger and hate, cheeks turning pale and lumps protruding in their throats, making it hard for them to swallow—that they are experiencing difficulty receiving it. Therefore, in telling them the truth, in love, without suppressing or distorting it, I sometimes find it necessary to restore them gently by prettying it up—adding to it sugar, spice, flowers, perfume, diamonds, pearls and lace, and all types of pleasant words that promote instruction to make it sweet to the soul and healing to the bones.

I know that, no matter what, I must tell the truth in Christ at all times—sometimes with fear—even if it means that I might become someone's enemy.

Therefore, always thinking of protecting them, I try to end a session of being truthful—even one that may be hurtful—on an encouraging, positive note, in order that people might not get offended, and may come to accept the truth a little easier. Although it is sometimes difficult for me to tell them the truth, in the end, I am set free, because no matter how much sweetness and beauty I try to add to it, I must speak the truth, and whether or not they accept it, or reject it, is not on me but on them. The Bible tells me that Jesus Christ, Himself, the Word of God, is the Truth (Jn 14:6). So, when people reject the truth, they are not rejecting me but the truth that they see in me, and in Jesus, which is the Word of God.

In telling people the truth, and in being kind—telling people what they need to hear, as opposed to telling them what they want to hear—I have learned, through my experiences, that sometimes people need to be corrected in order that they might come correct.

There have been several occasions when I have found it necessary to tell people with whom I have associated how I felt with regard to some of their faulty behaviors. To my surprise, many of the people who I thought would resent my rebuke have found it in their hearts—even several years later—to come back and tell me, "Thank you." They said that nobody had ever told them those things about themselves before. Because I opened my mouth in love, they were able to search their hearts and become wiser. All too often, people do not know about their shortcomings because no one is willing to correct, rebuke and encourage them with great patience and careful instruction, but, instead, withhold their rebuke in order to protect their reputation of being "nice." By doing so, in the end, they are not helping but hindering others from gaining wisdom.

There have been other times when those who I thought would appreciate my correction the most have ended up hating me, seeking revenge and holding grudges against me. I found that the only way that I would know the difference between the wise man and the fool is to rebuke them all. If my brothers and sisters get mad at me and start acting like fools, then I know in the future that I must withhold correction in order to preserve my life. But if they accept my correction, encouragement, training and rebuke, I know that they are wise and discerning, and are apt to accept more rebuke, only to become wiser. Either way, however, whether or not appreciation for my rebuking folk has been acknowledged, in the end, I know I will gain more favor for rebuking them than others who just want to appease them with a flattering tongue, telling them what they want to hear.

Many people—and I would even be bold enough to say that most people—do not speak the truth, but instead, teach their tongues to lie and to deceive. Oftentimes, when I ask people—my children, staff, friends, family, business folk, church folk—why certain inappropriate and noncompliant things have happened, I frequently hear excuses. Needless to say, even though people usually know right from wrong, they either pretend that they don't, or there is always an excuse given as to why they chose to do wrong, and usually, it is always someone else's fault. It is a given, for example, that when I ask each of my two daughters why they did something wrong, the first words that come out of their mouth is either, "You said..." or the name of their sibling, teacher or someone else.

It is as though people naturally want to blame everyone else for the things they do, and do not do, and as though no one wants to take responsibility for their own actions. Speaking for myself, my mind immediately searches for someone or something else to blame, besides myself, as it is a relief when I can project the issue off of myself, relieving myself of guilt, feelings of inadequacy and flaws.

Oftentimes, when we cannot come up with anyone or anything else to blame, we quickly find an excuse to support our wrongdoings, our sins. Excuses, however, if used too often, can become addictive because they afford us a legal, reasonable and acceptable escape route from doing what we should do, and in doing what we should not do. When we continuously give ourselves, others and God excuse after excuse, we are actually denying the truth—which is a form of lying. People get so caught up in giving excuses, they feel that when they give them, no matter what the wrongdoing, everybody is supposed to excuse their wrongdoing and go flying off into the great abyss, simply because they were given a worthless excuse.

Surprisingly, while reprimanding one of my employees—one who I considered to be responsible and possessed with common sense—for throwing her cigarette butts on the ground right outside the front door of my business, as opposed to putting them inside the ashtray, even after she had been previously verbally warned on several occasions and then finally written up, when I asked her why she continued to do it, not offering any excuses, her shocking reply was, "Just did; triflingness." Because she was so honest and didn't try to play with my intelligence by offering any excuses for her behavior, but instead came correct, first of all I couldn't help but laugh at her blunt and honest answer. Then I applauded her honesty and simply asked her to please not let it happen again. She genuinely apologized for throwing the cigarette butts on the ground, and assured me that she would not do it anymore; and she didn't. I find it easier to forgive and to understand people for their wrongdoings when they come correct, and speak the truth no matter what— even if it means that they are the one who is wrong.

Keep Your Excuse

When you don't want to do something
and you know
you're not going to do it anyway,
but you say yes because you're afraid to say no,
KEEP YOUR EXCUSE!

When you don't do your very best
and you know that it was within your control
to do so,
but you don't, because doing so
has no effect on your personal goals,
KEEP YOUR EXCUSE!

When you don't give,
but you know God has blessed you with the means,
when you have need of something,
who'll be your go-between?
KEEP YOUR EXCUSE!

When you don't teach, and the opportunity pre-
sents itself,
but you respond too late,
and instead, you allow folk to go fishing
without a fishing line and bait,
KEEP YOUR EXCUSE!

When you don't give back to the Lord
all that belongs to Him,
He's going to get it anyway,
so you might as well give in and
KEEP YOUR EXCUSE!

When you don't control your tongue,
don't blame it on menopause or PMS,
the damage has already been done,
and has taken its effect, so just apologize and
KEEP YOUR EXCUSE!

When you don't live and love
as the Lord has told you to,
then when this world has been said and done
and you've been asked why you do the things you
do, again,
KEEP YOUR EXCUSE!

Being without excuse, oftentimes, people try to present excuses to God for their sin, disobedience and ignorance, trying to play Him for a fool; saying things like they do not serve Him because they do not know Him. But God, having made plainly known, clearly seen and understood, even His invisible qualities—His eternal power and divine nature—refuses to know them, and thus turns them over to their sinful desires and depraved minds. Some people like to present the excuse for their not serving God: they did not know that the wrong that they were doing was sin. When Adam ate of the fruit of the Tree of the Knowledge of Good and Evil, the eyes of mankind were opened, and like God, we all know right from wrong. Still, some people use the excuse for their sinfulness that they do not know how to live a life from sin and come correct. But because Jesus came and spoke to us and showed us how to live and how to come correct, again, we have no excuse.

There was a long time span in my life when my ability to communicate openly was stunted by my fear of communicating with certain individuals of authority—my father, my teachers, my bosses, who were both male and female. I was like a scared pussycat shivering in the cold, when my bosses would just look my way, not to mention looking at, listening to and speaking with them, all except one of them. I had no fear of Milly, a woman of age and blessings, because I know, no matter what I did right or wrong, she loved, appreciated and accepted me for being me, and wasn't too proud to serve me by helping to teach me. She, being a good example for me, taught me good things: to love my husband and children—not that I had any at the time, but for those I would have in my future—to be self-controlled and pure, to be busy at home, to be kind, and to be subject to my husband.

Milly, in teaching me, didn't mind having her humanness exposed, if, by sharing her faults, it meant that my life could, in some way, be blessed. I have been blessed over the years to have been exposed to many such Millys in my life: my mother, aunts, family, friends and different women in the church. Because these women were taught to be reverent in the way they live; not slanderers or addicted to much wine, but teaching what is good, they were able to teach me, a younger woman, what I need to know in order for me to come to a place whereby I can live as an older woman should live by the time I am old. These Millys in my life taught me that people understand more about being human and more about the truth than they like to elude. And thus, communicating with them became easier for me.

Some people understand the nature of being human (that they, too, sin and fall short of the glory of God), but they pretend that they do not understand, so they will not be held accountable for shunning evil. They pretend also not to know the truth, when they do not feel that they want to be set free from sin. These people who deceive themselves into believing that they are beyond being human and beyond hearing the truth actually neither know, nor understand, anything. They walk around in darkness and all the foundations of the earth are shaken. They who reject the truth for any reason are senseless fools.

We all make mistakes, and at some time in our lives will trespass against someone else. When Jesus was teaching us how we should pray, He asked that God forgive us our debts as we forgive our debtors (Mt 6:12). When people are morally indebted to us, all we want is for them to come correct and earnestly apologize for their wrongdoing and not repeat the offense. Instead, however, most people try to cover up their wrongdoings; oftentimes blaming others and/or coming up with excuses or lies to support their wrongdoings. Sometimes, apologies are made just to smooth over a situation in order to avoid ongoing strife, but the person apologizing is not godly sorrowful for the hurtful thing that they have done, thinking that simply saying the words *I'm sorry* without changing their minds or their hearts gets them off the hook.

One day, my then four-year-old daughter did something to upset my older daughter. I told her that she needed to go and apologize to her big sister. She went into my older daughter's room and said, "I'm sorry, Desirée." Desirée immediately screamed out to me, "Mom, she didn't say it like she meant it." I then told Alyssa to go and say it like you mean it. Alyssa went back into Desirée's room and, putting her hands on her hips, in a sassy tone of voice, she said, "Like I mean it, Desirée." Alyssa was no more sorrowful in her heart than many of us are, when we only apologize with our mouth. Even when we apologize to God for our sins, sometimes we are not sorrowful in our hearts, but He sees our hearts and knows when we are truly sorry and when we are just using lip service.

It seems as though one of the hardest things for people to do is to apologize. I believe the main reason people have such a difficult time apologizing is that no one wants to humble themselves. To humble one's self means to become submissive; to swallow one's pride and to surrender oneself to another. Ephesians 5:21 says that we are to submit to one another, out of reverence for Christ. The Scriptures further tell us that the Lord saves the humble, guides them in what is right, gives them grace and esteems and exalts them. The problem is that inasmuch as God wants to save, guide into what is right, give grace, esteem and exalt us, not many of us are willing to humble ourselves, and...

Just Apologize

Can't you just say you're sorry?
Can't you admit you're wrong?
Why don't you come down from your high horse
and stop being so headstrong?

Why can't you just say you're sorry?
Take a sigh and apologize.
What do you think will be said of you
when it's your turn to be eulogized?

Go on and get it out.
You'll feel better when it's said and done.
Just because you were first to say sorry the last time,
it doesn't mean the other person has won.

Instead, you'll come out the winner
because you would have humbled yourself
by submitting to another;
putting your pride up on a shelf.

There'll be a time when we all must be humble;
a time when every knee shall bow.
God is giving us an opportunity to practice
falling to our knees right now.

Oftentimes even though we might be willing to apologize, we are hesitant because we are afraid that people might not accept our apologies, and forgive us of our wrongdoings. We know that although we are willing to humble ourselves, other people might just refuse to humble themselves, and accept our apologies, but would rather hold grudges so that they can maintain their anger in order to keep ammunition that can be used against us for the next time that we might do them wrong. Some people may be hesitant to forgive others because their ego is boosted when people do them wrong, as they feel more powerful because being victimized in the relationship gives them more control. They like to be in a position of being owed something by others, and thus are quick to use this opportunity of victimization to gain pity, promote guilt, get attention and make others jump through hoops until they have earned their way back into their hearts. Still others go around telling everybody else that a certain person has wronged them in order to turn other people against the person who has done the wrongdoing.

We cannot be responsible for whether or not a person accepts our apologies, but we, as God's children, must always come correct and ask for forgiveness. To come correct means that we must repent of our sins to every man against whom we have sinned, as well as to God. We must, however, look to the Lord to restore us, and not man, as it is He who forgives our sins. When a person does not accept our heartfelt apology, then that is between them and their god. But as for us, because, when we repent of our sins and ask God to forgive us, then we are set free of our sins and become free, indeed.

What a Friend

*Beware of your friends; do not trust your brothers.
For every brother is a deceiver, and every friend
a slanderer. Friend deceives friend, and no one
speaks the truth. (Jer 9:4–5a)*

I believe that I am not alone when I say that it is important for me to have positive friendships in my life with people with whom I share various commonalities; people with whom I can have fun—talking and thinking, laughing and crying, acting silly and being serious, eating and drinking, singing and dancing, going places and staying home, sharing memories, thoughts and ideas. There are times in my life, however, when I feel as though I have no real friends in my life, and deep down inside, I yearn for one. I believe most of us want someone in our lives whom we can truly call our friend. Because of the fact that I take my responsibility as a friend very seriously and that I am very choosy about those who I call my friends, there have been numerous occasions in my life when while telling someone about something I had gone through, I have had to back up and correct myself when I inaccurately labeled someone as "my friend." Because in some way or another, they proved themselves not to be a true friend to me, I had to re-label them as "someone who I once thought was my friend."

At this point in my life—no offense to anyone who may consider him- or herself to be my friend—but there are only a few people who I can truly call my friends—and even they happen to be family members. Although, like in any other relationship, each of these few family members of mine, those who I can truly call my friends, has let me down at one point or another, when all has been said and done, they have proved themselves to be a friend to me because we have a mutually respectful relationship, which is based on unconditional love. They know my ins and my outs. They have taken the time to know me and to love me, in spite of me. They always have my best interest at heart, as they protect my heart from anything that would be hurtful to me.

Some people throw that word *friend* around as though it is a word that they use to describe *all* of their associations. Oftentimes, they quickly identify other people as their friend, telling them what a great friend they are. Then they expect you to obligate yourself to a friendship with them, just because they have identified you as their friend. Because they know that "friends" is not something you say but something you do, they ask you for something—a special favor—perhaps a ride, a loan, the answers to your homework, a place to stay, etc. They equate your friendship with how much you are willing to do for them, so they keep asking you for more and more favors; giving you plenty of opportunities to prove your friendship to them. When you see the game they are playing with you, and you stop playing, then they go and find other friends.

Inasmuch as we all may want good friends, I believe, based on my experiences, that very few can truly say that we have been a good friend to others; one who, in every possible situation, has loved and has given of him- or herself unselfishly; one who has never participated in gossip and slander; one who always listens to the cares and concerns of his or her friends and offers help when possible; one who believes in his or her friends, building them up when they are torn down and when necessary, sacrificing their own needs for those of their friends.

One of the ironies of friendship is that inasmuch as we all want good, close friends in our lives to whom we can talk, share our thoughts, feelings, experiences, memories and our love, many of us have become hesitant to completely opening up to the notion of friendship because we have been hurt worse by people who have called themselves our friends than by those who have not. Because we know that everyone who calls him- or herself a friend is not necessarily a friend, we know that we must exert extreme caution when choosing our friends, and to keep our guard up. We refrain from telling people too much about ourselves early on in the relationship because we know that some people store up weapons against us based on knowledge that they have of us. And when we start to argue or fall out with them, everything we ever did that they even thought was wrong comes out, and is used against us.

When we allow people to enter our lives, homes, hearts, minds and emotions, we make ourselves vulnerable to anything that they have in their hearts to bring upon us. If they want to know all of our business so that they can slander our name and tell all of our deepest, darkest secrets, then we become available for that. If their intentions are to get close to us so they can try to steal our stuff, our mates or our identity, then, in dealing with them, we set ourselves up for that. If they want to hang around us to leach off of us for money, special favors and things, then by being around them, we avail ourselves of that, too. If they get close enough to us, they have the potential for hurting us to the extent where sometimes our very lives can be jeopardized. Friends can make us or break us. Everything that we have, we stand to lose in the name of a friend, including our reputations, our money, material things, other relationships, our morals, our self-respect and yes, even our very lives.

Another of the ironies of friendships is that as hurtful as they can be, they can also bring us much joy and fond memories. A good, Christian friend can offer us prayer and encouragement, they can help us to discover ourselves in the Lord and to stay on the right spiritual path. Unfortunately, these days, even a good, Christian friend is hard to find. I knew we were all in trouble when I heard my pastor say in church while preaching one of his prophetic sermons, that it was difficult for him to find people of integrity in his circle of friends. Before I knew it, I screamed out to him, "Not you, too, Pastor!".

As important as it is for me to have positive friendships in my life, I am not willing to sacrifice all that I stand to lose for the sake of my friends, and by the same token, none are willing to lose all they have for me; therefore, truth be told, when I really think about it, I have no friends because no man is able to be all that I need in a friend, but Jesus. Each and every one of my friends has let me down and has shown themselves not to be a friend to me at some time or another. I have had friends who have slandered my name, told other people things they promised me they would not tell, lied to me while swearing to God that they were telling me the truth, borrowed money from me and never paid me back, then found reasons to stop speaking to me so they could have an excuse to be out of my life, accused me of trying to steal their man, friends who didn't do what they said they were going to do, refused to be there for me when I needed them (or gave me an attitude for me even asking) and threw our friendship away without even giving me a reason why.

Inasmuch as these friends have shown themselves not to be friends to me, at some point or another, others have shown themselves to be friends to me. These friends have called to see about me in the midst of my trials, treated me out to a meal, sent me a card or gave me encouraging words at times in my life when I've been at my lowest, spoken well of me to others, brought me fun and laughter, helped me with my children and encouraged me to do things God's way.

There have been occasions in my life when I have found it necessary to make a clean sweep of all of my friends so that I could be by myself for a while, without any friends, in order that I might evaluate all of my friendships to determine which ones I wanted to keep in my life and which I should let go. Although it has been very difficult to let go of some of my friends because of the unique and intimate qualities that we share, I knew it was in my best interest spiritually, emotionally, mentally, physically, financially and/or socially that I move on. Moving on from relationships can feel somewhat like a death because it usually means that you are no longer physically present with that person. But because it may become necessary for the health of one's overall psyche, sometimes, for our own good, it is best that we just move on. ◊

Move On

Good bye, familiar
Hello, unfamiliar
New horizons echo my name
New dreams await my sleep
Doors open, others close
Confirming prayers and ears to hear
Lead my destiny

Paths previously unavailable to me
Have once again been cleared
Stumbling blocks along my journey
That were once in my way
May have caused me to trip;
But I never fell
My posture remains upright; my strides, wide

Higher heights which are more visible to me
In their array of bright colors
Matched with those of a rainbow
Dance at the city gate
Demanding my attention
Their arms flapping in the wind
In all directions
As though the course were mine to choose

I see my life through the eyes of God
His reflection ever present in me
I see my life through my own eyes
Which are looking up again
Not out at my situation
Nor back with regrets
Not down as if needing security with each step
But up for answers, strength, faith...everything

Much obliged that I should be released
From predators gnawing at my joy
The splashes of wind beat freedom against my face
My walls are back down again
Love has become my reason
Space is mine to claim
My existence or nonexistence in it
Consideration finally given to my wishes

Burdens sometimes grow heavy
I must travel light and take along
Only that which is necessary to sustain me for my
journey
Leaving behind anger, blame, bitterness, guilt
and shame
And always packing and carrying with me
Lessons learned, forgiveness, wisdom,
Patience, understanding, The Word of Truth

Progressively dumping one set of issues
For a healthier set of issues

Giving the gifts of grace and mercy
Without prejudgment or resentment
Being about peace
Praying for those who forsake me
Refraining from taking God's revenge from Him
Or thoughts, thereof
Openly and honestly communicating
Advancing others, as I advance
Teaching, as I am taught
I MOVE ON!

Inasmuch as I have tried to be a good friend to each and every one of my friends, if you asked each of them about how good of a friend I have been, although most would say that my positive aspects far outweigh my negative ones, similarly, I'll bet each of them would say that in some way, I, too, have let them down.

We all want a perfect friend, but none of us are a perfect friend, in return. Through my personal experiences, I've learned that friends will often let you down. We sometimes place so much value on our friendships, and eventually, we find that the people who we have called our friends are the ones who have ended up deceiving and hurting us the most. I have had many friends that I thought I could trust to love me unconditionally, but as time went on, somehow, something happened that caused one of us to either terminate the relationship or decrease hope in it.

There has been only one friend that I ever had who has never let me down. That friend is Jesus. When I established a true friendship with Him, doing what He commands of me, I discovered that He is a friend who will love me at all times and always be there for me.

There was a time in my life when I thought that as long as I was being a true friend to others, sharing with *God's people* who were in need and practicing hospitality, that they, in return, would be a true friend to me. I welcomed anyone in my home who wanted to be my friend. As a matter of fact, my home was so overdecorated with items that displayed the word "WELCOME" that one might think that my home was designed especially for visitors. I enjoyed meeting new people and offering hospitality to them; fellowshipping with them in my home, preparing meals for them and making them feel comfortable, and did so without grumbling. Like Job, my door was always open to the traveler. I wanted to do good to all people, especially to those who belong to the family of Believers.

Come, Be Refreshed!

If I have found favor in your eyes,
do not pass your servant by.
Come on in and take a shower.
Rest your eyes until the morning hour.
Let me get you something good to eat,
a seat, so you can relax your feet.
Come, be relaxed, before going on your way,
since you've come to your servant on this day.

As much as I always wanted people to feel welcomed and "at home" when they came into my house, there have been times when it was not convenient for me to accept them into my home because perhaps it was not clean or my money was low and I didn't have the best food in my refrigerator, or I had to grab a clean towel from the dryer to give to them, but even still, I had to set aside my own embarrassment and let my guests know that in spite of my shortcomings, if they were able to excuse my present living conditions, still, they were welcomed. ◂

Just Down-Home Folk

We may not roll out the red carpet
when you come into our home,
but when you gather with us,
may you never feel alone.
Our home is sometimes messy,
but we can always make some space.
Don't want to feel uneasy,
so just please excuse the place.

If you're hungry, tired or thirsty,
we cannot read your mind;
so you'll have to let us know,
and I'm sure that we can find
some food, some drink, a blanket and pillow
for you to rest your mind.
We're just down-home folk;
not trying to be anything more.
So go on and make yourself at home,
the minute we open our door.

Admittedly, there have been other instances, when, without any notice, my doorbell would ring. Tiptoeing my way to the peephole, there have been times when my door looked better shut than open, and I decided not to be hospitable. Although I believe that it is important for us to be hospitable to one another, we have to be very careful about to whom we decide to open our door. At one time, I thought, as a Christian, that my door was supposed to be opened to everyone. However, life, and careful study of God's Word, has taught me differently.

Inasmuch as we may want a good friend, Jesus, whose door is always open for us, wants to be a friend to us all. When we follow Him by doing what He commands, then during times in our lives when we feel discouraged, and need encouragement, Jehovah-Nissi (God, our banner) will give it to us. When we are stressed out and need someone to talk to us and listen to us, Jehovah-Shalom (God of our peace) will always be there to hear us, to listen to us and to talk to us. When we need a warm hug, Jehovah-Shammah (God who is there) will send someone whom we may least expect, to give us that hug that we need. When we need some money to pay our bills, and we don't have a clue from where it is coming, Jehovah-Jireh (God, our provider) will always make a way for us and provide for us that which we need. When we need someone to encourage us to do that which is good, Jehovah-Tsidkenu (God of our righteousness) will encourage us to do that which is good.

Naturally, of course, the friends that God would want us to have are godly friends—those who are there for us when we need them spiritually, mentally, emotionally, physically and even financially; friends who encourage us and build us up, helping us to feel good about who we are and who we were designed to be; friends who bear their own burdens to the best of their ability. We must, therefore, wait on God to send to us such godly friends—even if it means, in the meantime, that for a season, we must be without a friend. Because, as Believers, we are not to yoke ourselves with unbelievers (in any relationship capacity, as far as I am concerned, including as associates, friends, spouses, business partners, employers, employees and any other type of relationship), we must be very careful and in constant prayer about those with whom we deal, eat, sleep, date, marry, work, allow in our homes, visit, do business, fellowship and associate—even those to whom we give.

Pray—Even In Your Giving

As a child, I was trained up
in the way I should go.
I was provided with all that was needed
to help me to grow
to be a God-fearing, people-loving child
of the Most High King;
acknowledging His presence
in each and every thing.

My mom taught me to be well mannered;
to reach out and to give.
I sought to please God
by the way that I lived.
For some reason, every time folk needed me,
I thought I should be there.
It didn't matter
who, what, when or where.

I thought I was doing
my Father's will,
but my cup was getting empty,
while theirs was being filled.
Every time I loaned out money,
nobody paid me back.
They took my kindness for weakness
and counted it as lack.

They stripped me of things
that were near and dear to me.
Their hearts were not touched
when I begged them for mercy.
Although I made them fully aware
of how they let me down,
they didn't understand my pain
until I turned the situation around.

I had to break down and ask them,
"What if I did that to you?"
"How would you feel if you went through
all that you put me through?"
For their own self-centered reasons,
they were able to understand
the nonsense they put me through
when I lended them a hand.

Even still, they hung on to their selfishness,
not paying the debts they owe—
not one of them responding a bit
to the love that I had showed.
My mom warned me that, "The same folk you
meet going up,
you'll meet them coming down."
She told me, "That which goes around
will surely come around."

My father said, "That which you sow,
you shall also reap."
I thought about their stony hearts,
and for them, I began to weep.
Like my big brother, Jesus, and through Him,
I pray,
"Father, forgive them, for they know not what
they do.
Then I leave it alone because
vengeance, grace and mercy belong to you."

As I start to look inside myself to figure out
the lesson that needed to be learned
for all the tears that I shed, the things that I lost
and the strife I may have earned,
I had to look at why I allowed myself
to be treated in that way;
why I would let people get over on me,
and do to me whatever they may.

I had to explore the reasons that were deep in me,
why I always felt so free to give.
Then I looked at the life of Jesus Christ
as an example of how He lived.
He was all about love and giving—
He gave His very life.
Yet even through His giving,
He was faced with undue strife.

I learned that if I couldn't afford to give it away,
then I should not loan it out.
I no longer put my trust in any man,
just to have to find out what they're all about.
I started to put my trust in God, and before I give,
or yoke myself with man in any way,
I go to God and seek His will,
as it is Him that I want to obey.

As a submissive wife goes to her husband,
and a respectful husband, to his wife,
that's how I go to my Father,
even in my giving, to have a happier life.
I'm not supposed to cast my pearls to pigs,
nor to dogs, those things that are sacred.
I have to make sure that even in my giving,
I'm being spirit-led.

Just because someone asks me for something,
it doesn't mean I have to say, "Yes."
As long as I'm doing my Father's will,
I'm doing my very best.
Then, when I give, it's not about me
and the ones to whom I give;
It's about my relationship with Jesus Christ,
and the way He wants me to live. •

Because no man is perfect, and not one of us can be
trusted at all times, we have to be very careful about

who we are willing to have in our lives. The first person who we cannot always trust, but with whom we need to strive to establish a trusting relationship, is ourselves. We need to be faithful and accountable to ourselves and always true to who we say we are and to that which we say we will do. We need to make sure that all of our relationships and all of our dealings are true, and that everything we say is truthful. We need to be true to our thoughts, emotions, desires and feelings and not be in denial about anything. We must also be true to our Lord, our responsibilities and our purpose.

Once we acknowledge the fact that only God is able to be a true friend to us, and that even we ourselves are not always a true friend to ourselves, then we begin to understand that if we associate ourselves close enough with individuals for a time, that all people will, at some time, let us down. Once we accept this reality, we can stop expecting everyone to be a true friend to us and place our focus, instead, on being a true friend to ourselves, others, and most important, to God, by believing in Him and doing what He commands. We are to be a friend to everyone, regardless of how we are treated by others, just as Jesus was a friend to us all, as demonstrated by His laying down His life for us.

While living in this world, we are not to be friends with the terrors of darkness, but must be very careful about our associations and about those whom we regard as our friends. We are not to be spiritually adulterous; friends *of* the world whose prince, now standing condemned, is satan, but are commanded to come out of the world and be separate from unbelievers who love the world, not allowing ourselves to be polluted by the world. We who love the Lord do not love the world, anything in it, or anything that comes from it; its cravings of sinful man, the lust of his eyes and the boasting of what he has and does. Because the world hates the Father, who testifies that what it does is evil, they hate the Spirit of God in those of us who are Children of God, because our spirit testifies with His Spirit.

If we are friends of the world, then we are being an enemy of God, and therefore, are not His friend. The Bible identifies various types of people of the world with whom we are not to associate. Some of them include: those who are hot-tempered and easily angered, people with many friends, people who talk too much, a gossip, those who call themselves a brother but are sexually immoral, greedy, idolaters, slanderers, drunkards, swindlers, those who are lovers of self and of money, people who are boastful, proud, abusive, disobedient to their parents, ungrateful, unholy, without love, unforgiving, without self-control, brutal, not lovers of the good, treacherous, rash, conceited, lovers of pleasure rather than lovers of God—

having a form of godliness but denying its power. As a matter of fact, 2 Timothy 3:5 tells us to have *nothing* to do with them. Instead, we are to live righteously and to associate ourselves in the company of God, and with other Believers who love righteousness and hate wickedness.

Matthew 12:33–35 explains how we are known by our fruit, whether good or bad. People with good fruit are those who walk in love, joy, peace, patience, kindness, goodness, faithfulness (Gal 5:22), while people with bad fruit are controlled by the sinful nature and bear fruit for death (Rom 7:5). Because the Bible clearly tells us not to hang out with bad people, then, without condemning or judging folk, I have found it necessary to intensely screen the people with whom I choose to associate. In my walk with God, I found that it sometimes becomes necessary for me to let go of some of my friends and associations because a point is reached in the relationship when it is no longer in my best interest to continue in it—usually because of a reason outlined in the above checklist of folk with whom my Father told me I am not to hang. There are even occasions whereby, when I look around, it appears as though I don't have any friends at all.

At Times I Feel Like
I Have No Friends

At times I feel like I have no friends
because I stopped picking up the phone and all
the pieces after midnight and listening
to the selfish reasons for their calls.

At times I feel like I have no friends
because I no longer sit around
listening to folk raising themselves up,
while putting me down.

At times I feel like I have no friends
because instead of being the Bank of the Destitute,
I, instead, teach folk how to wait on the Lord,
as I have had to do.

At times I feel like I have no friends
because I no longer choose be used as a buffer
to take up empty space
just because there is no other.

At times I feel like I have no friends
because I no longer go out with them to get men
who lie in wait to choose me for the night
to commit immoral sins.

At times I feel like I have no friends
because I would rather pay for just my way,
and not for everyone else who accompanies me,
because they can never pay.

At times I feel like I have no friends
because I'm happy and content being with just me,
learning from my Father, how to be
the best friend to me
that I can possibly be.

Inasmuch as I like to talk to and hang out with a good friend, sharing good times, because my primary goal in life is to one day live in a most beautiful mansion, as I store up my treasures in heaven, oftentimes, I would prefer to spend my time with my one and only true friend, Jesus. I therefore seek to gain every possible moment in quiet commune with God. Additionally, because there aren't many people with whom I like to spend my time enough to give up my intimate time with my Father, when I finally do decide to give up some of my time to be with other people, they have to be very special people. Therefore, the godly friends that I have, and those that I will have in the future, are valuable blessings for my life, and although they do and will fall short, they will also bring good words and good deeds to my life.

The Need To Work

Then He said to His disciples, "The harvest is plentiful but the workers are few." (Mt 9:37)

There is plenty of work to be done on our land, but it seems these days that no one wants to work for his living. Everyone wants to take easy ways out; get-rich-quick schemes, opening one's own business with thoughts of being able to avoid hard work, swindling people, selling drugs, gambling and other illegal activities. When it comes to our finances, we all want to "arrive" but few of us want to accept the hard work and all the challenges involved with getting there. Many who go into business for themselves are disgruntled because they soon find out that they have to work hard in order to make ends meet. Even if they hire employees to do the work, they lose out on money, and they lose out on quality, because nobody is able to do the job right, as if they had done it. Very few people seem to enjoy their work, as evident by the poor service and rude behavior that I constantly encounter in dealing with people who are "doing their jobs" out there in the business world.

God, to whom dominion belongs, and who rules over the nations, was losing some of us and the quality of our work. I thank Him that He decided to come to His place of business, because none of us were able to do the job right. He came to help us to live abundantly by teaching us to do what He commands us to do, and by showing us how to do them by practicing them. He didn't belittle us for not doing our jobs correctly. He didn't insult us, even though we insulted Him. Instead, He got down and dirty with us and endured some horrific things for our sake—even death—so that we could keep His business running.

I've heard it said (and I even say it myself from time to time) that "business is business." Well, not anymore! Business used to be business—or at least it acted as if it was. But now, based on my experiences with the business world, business is not respected the way it once was, because the world is full of disgruntled workers and it seems that no one wants to do his job. Everyone wants to be doing something else. People do not appear to be content in their present situations, and often claw at others to try to bring them down. People are not putting aside their personal attitudes and emotions for the sake of business, respecting one another, taking pride in their company and fearing job loss, the way they once did. Instead, business has become a cesspool for people's inadequacies, insecurities, lies, frustrations, lawsuits and negative attitudes. ✦

As a writer, I am blessed to have the opportunity to spend much of my time in solitude with my Father. However, even still, often I find it necessary to deal with people in the business world; either by phone, in person or by e-mail. One day I hired a handyman to do some work in my home. He came to my house at ten in the morning, and when he arrived I was already in a bad mood. He asked me if I had gone out on that day, because he couldn't understand why I was in such a bad mood so early in the morning. I explained to him that although I had not left my home, I had spoken with several businesses on the telephone and that sometimes it is not necessary for me to even leave the house for people to get on my nerves, but that all I have to do is pick up the phone.

I have held positions in all spectrums of the business world: employee, supervisor, employer and so-called "valued customer," and in all spectrums I have experienced so much mistreatment, hate, inconsideration and disrespect that sometimes I feel that if I had it my way, I would never have anything to do with the "business world" again. As an employee, I've dealt with "valued customers" who took their frustrations out on me merely because I was following my company's policies and procedures. I have had supervisors who have tried to unnecessarily exert their power and control over me, those who constantly re-design their policies to benefit themselves, increase my job duties, and those who have made promises to me that they did not fulfill. I have also dealt with co-workers who have tried to make me feel bad for doing a good job because I took my work seriously and worked hard, as opposed to goofing off like the rest of them; thus, *making* them look bad.

As a supervisor, I have dealt with managers who didn't support me but hid themselves off upstairs in their offices all day, telling me to call them when I need them; then, when I call them, they are nowhere around, leaving me to deal with the *wolves* all by my-self. These same managers, who were constantly try-ing to intimidate me by making me feel as though my position was in jeopardy if I failed to complete all of the duties that they'd assigned to me, were constantly loading *their* work on me. I've had to deal with man-agers who didn't recognize me for the work I did but only focused on the work that was not done because I was too busy completing so many of the other dom-inant, extraneous demands of the job.

Also, as a supervisor, I have dealt, unfortunately, in numerous situations, with insubordinate employ-ees who, for one reason or another, refused to fulfill the obligations of their position, then would do all they could to try to sabotage my position. They would envy my position as their supervisor, and although they seemed to accept my instruction with their eyes and their ears, they would not accept it with their mouths, but instead, would talk behind my back about what they're not going to do. Additionally, there were those who were subordinate to me, who would try to butter me up so that I would show them favoritism by allowing them to get away with doing things that they weren't supposed to do, or not to do the things that they were supposed to do.

At one time, it was boasted that the customer was always right. And even though we weren't, people in business tried to please and appease us to make us feel as though we were; just so they could keep us as their customers. Now it seems that they could care less about whether or not we return as customers, and although they are the ones who do all of the inputting of the data, the computers are always right. In order for me to be relieved of that which I am being accused by them—not paying my bill on time, for example—the hardship of proving that I did, in fact, do what was expected of me is placed in my lap and, even when I am not at fault, and am not being paid to do the job, in order for me to maintain my credit, I have to be the one to dig up my bank statements, make phone calls, fax information and the like.

Each and every one of us has his own personal life, and thus, our personal business, in which to manage;

spiritually, mentally, emotionally, financially, morally, legally, socially and in every other way. Many of us say that we want to be in business for ourselves, but we do not even handle the affairs of our personal business efficiently, effectively and responsibly. Everyone who goes into business should not, because many people either do not want to, or they do not know how to, handle the demands of a business. Because of their lack, the customers end up suffering; we have to wait in their long lines, be understanding when they run out of product or pay higher prices because the next closest place is much farther away. Granted, in most situations we go into business to make money. We look for "the big way out"; the way out of spending too much time making money, and too little time spending it. We want the big way out, but we want the easy way out; the way out of investing all that is required of us, in order for us to acquire and to sustain our own business in an honest, caring and serving manner. In short, many of us want our own business, but in many cases we are ill equipped to faithfully handle the demands of having our own business in such areas as our loyalty, honesty, maturity, self-restraint, judgment, professionalism, responsibility, accountability, ability, sociality, communication and the like.

Even though we might possess all that is necessary for us to start a business, oftentimes we do not have that which is required of us to sustain a business; the desire, drive, passion, perseverance, physical energy, finances, knowledge and support necessary for us to do so. Although we all are most likely lacking in one area or another of our personal lives, some folk are ill equipped to correctly handle the demands of their own personal business, let alone the demands of any business outside of their own. If we are not being faithful to properly manage our personal lives, then why would God put us in charge of more? To have one's own business means that one must work hard— perhaps even harder than one would for someone else. All too often, people who are in business fail to correctly handle their business. All too often, I must, in some way, pay.

Mind Your Business

Why is it that when you mess up,
it is I who must—in some way—repay
when I'm dealing with businesses?
Let me break something in your store,
make a late payment,
or want something more
than what I bargained for.
See how my pockets get emptied,
while yours get full.

But let one of your people make a mistake,
and still, again, it is I
who must make the sacrifice
in order for your wrong to get right.
I am the one who must
drive my car back to your place of business,
using my gas,
my postage stamps and my time
to explain your mistakes
but not getting paid one dime
for doing so,
while you do,
all while still not receiving what I wanted,
when and how I wanted to.
Why must I pay for both

your mistakes and mine?
I wish you'd mind your business,
then I wouldn't have to.

Don't you advertise your business
so that you can get customers?
Or do you even want them?
When you get them, why don't you tend to them
like they're valuable and like you want them to stay,
instead of acting as though they're in the way?
When you see us coming, you say,
"Oh man, here comes more work!"
Please don't be upset with me for demanding
that you deliver all that you say you do.

You see that the color of my skin is brown,
and that I am a woman possessing
many questions and money.
Then you want to charge me more
than you would someone else—
thinking I won't know any better.
But will you? That's up to you!
I wouldn't, though, if I were you.
You'd better mind your business
and treat me fair
because my Father is aware
of everything you do.

I don't always have time to go behind you
to make sure that you treat me right.
But I serve a God who hates anyone who deals
dishonestly.
So, if this is you, you have my God to answer to.
Do what it is you're supposed to do;
and not only when people are watching you.
Your work is your lot;
it is something that you are responsible for
doing well—
no matter what your position.
You have a contract to provide a service.
Be faithful over the little things
so you can be trusted to rule over much.
Take responsibility for doing your best by
going beyond the call of duty, and not beneath it.
Mind your own business
And take care of all that is assigned to you,
as you do that which only you
were put here to do.

All too often, when people have businesses, in order for them not to have to be the only one handling the demands of the business, they hire employees. Unfortunately, many do not even come correct and treat people right in their personal lives, so why would God want them to be in charge of people in any other capacity? 1 Peter 5:2–3 says that we are to be shepherds of God's flock that is under our care, *serving* as overseers—not because we must, but *because we are willing,* as God wants us to be; not greedy for money, but eager to serve; not lording it over those entrusted to us, but being examples to the flock. Since God gave us different gifts of grace, everyone does not have the gift of serving (Rom 12: 6–7), and therefore, everyone is not in a position to shepherd, to serve willingly and eagerly and to be examples.

If we are to serve, shepherd and set the example, then we, ourselves, must be spiritually, mentally, emotionally, financially, socially and morally sound. Whatever qualities we expect in our employees, we, ourselves, must demonstrate as employers. We must be honest, fair, dependable and hardworking if we expect our employees to be the same. Similarly, Jesus Himself, the Good Shepherd, who came to serve, made an example of Himself when He demonstrated His love for us, in that while we were yet sinners, He died for us so that we could have eternal life. As business owners with Believers (God's flock) under our care, we are expected to demonstrate our love by serving our brothers as though we are giving life. If we keep the attitude that the reason for our work, both physically and in the kingdom, is so that we can serve those in need, then the focus of our work becomes more about others and not ourselves. •

As God works in us to will and to act according to His good purpose, because of our love for our brothers, we become willing to serve them. Then, because we are willing, we serve them with eagerness, out of our love for God. We work without complaining and arguing, and thus become workers who are blameless and pure because we know that our labor is not in vain. As we serve our brothers, our employees and our customers, we are careful not to be greedy or lord over those entrusted to us. Therefore we do not take advantage of a hired man who is poor and needy, nor do we trample on or oppress him.

Nowadays, everyone in business seems to be frustrated with everyone else; employers with employees, employees with employers, supervisors with their managers and subordinate workers, businesses with customers, and customers with businesses. The very reason that man was created—his purpose for being on the earth—was so that he would work the ground that God created. God then decided that it was not good for man to be alone, so He decided to make woman, a suitable helper for him. His original plan was for man to live in His presence in the beautiful Garden of Eden, but when Adam and Eve ate of the fruit of the Tree of Knowledge of Good and Evil, the tree of death, He cast them out of the garden and away from His presence. Because of man's disobedience, God cursed the ground with thorns and thistles, and through painful toil, man has been made to eat of it all the days of his life by the sweat of his brow until he returns back to it.

Just like rebelling children who are punished by their parents, both men and women are trying all they can to avoid their punishments that God handed down to them. Men, who were originally designed only to dress and keep the garden, naturally rebel against their punishment of having to eat their food by the sweat of their brow from the ground cursed with thorns and thistles, through painful toil, and are doing all they can to avoid their punishment of working long and hard, by being lazy and getting off as easy as possible; lollygagging and playing. Poverty is at an all-time high; not because there is no work available in this land of plenty known as America, but often because people are lazy, merely talkers and not hard workers, lovers of sleep and of pleasure.

Women, men's helpers, are not only trying to avoid helping men to work hard, but they too are doing all they can to avoid the punishments that God handed down to them for eating the fruit; increased pain in childbearing and our desire being for our husbands. God's primary goal throughout history is for man to return back into His presence. He first made provision for man to be restored back into His presence by giving him laws and commandments for him to follow, which no man did. Then, since no man was righteous and because of God's love for us, He sent His only Son to this world so that we might believe on Him and have everlasting life. Through Christ's death on the cross, by believing in Him as Savior and Lord of our lives, we now have an opportunity to be restored back to God's presence. ❧

Let's Both Go Back!

When we met, you declared me bone of your bone
and flesh of your flesh.
Yes, I knew better, but you,
having personally heard from God, knew best.
We both fell short by eating of the forbidden fruit,
choosing it over the rest.

We were both wrong. I was tricked by satan,
and you were tricked by me.
Have you truly forgiven me
for coercing you into being deceived?
I chose to trust satan, but it was me
to whom you listened and whom you chose
to believe.

You tried to put the blame on me, and even today,
I believe you still look at me that way.
When God passed out His punishment on us,
did you want me to stay?
Or did you want Him to be rid of me once and
for all,
on that fateful day?

Because I was made from you,
it was expected of you to leave your mom and dad.

You're still at home with your mom right now,
perhaps thinking of it as a fad.
You call yourself a man, but haven't left home,
and wives, you've already had.

You were expected to work the ground for your food,
to the sweat of your brow,
but look at who's bringing in more than half
the money
to support our families now!
You escape work through your irresponsibility,
disability checks
and other means that are or are not allowed.

Your manhood has become meaningless to us,
as our womanhood has, for you.
I guess that's why many women are getting
fed up and are through
expecting men to do what it is
that the Lord God expects them to do.

We were put here to be your help-mate,
please forgive us for steering you wrong.
We both fell short of God's glory
because we're both guilty of being headstrong.
But God gave us another chance so let's both go
back—to the garden—
where we both belong.

We all want the harvest of hard work, but not many of us, male or female, want to work hard in order to get the harvest—because our minds are not on our work but on other things. The minds of men and women are on different ways that they can avoid working hard, and instead, they think about lollygagging, chilling out and playing with (and without) their grown-up toys.

In order for us to teach people not to allow themselves to be controlled by life's pleasures, we need to give them knowledge that will help them to persevere and be self-controlled, living godly lives; not loaded down with sins and swayed by all kinds of evil desires. MOST OF ALL, WE MUST SET THE EXAMPLE BY DOING WHAT IS GOOD. In our teaching, we must show integrity, seriousness and soundness of speech that cannot be condemned, so that those who oppose us may be ashamed because they have nothing bad to say about us. Then, when they become older, it will be more likely that they can be taught to be temperate, worthy of respect, self-controlled and sound in faith, in love and in endurance.

All too often, we want to dismiss the fact that in most cases we must work hard and diligently, in order for us to have nice things. We are so quick to quit a job as opposed to staying there, growing with a company and working out our frustrations and making the workplace a better place for all. Instead, we would rather sue the company for job stress, collect unemployment or make up other excuses to get on disability or workers' compensation just so we can get out of doing what we've been hired to do. We take our aggressions out on our employers because we have to go to work to make *our* ends meet; we steal from them because they have more money than we do; we lie to them about why we don't report to work; we cheat on our time cards and retaliate against them when they won't give us a day off or raise our pay; all because we don't want to work.

Elevate Your Mind

You say you deserve to be "the boss,"
but you don't respect your own.
When your supervisor tells you what to do,
you tell her that you're grown.
They treat you like a slave, you say,
when they tell you to get to work!
Who's the slave if they have to pry you out of the restroom
every hour—like clockwork?

You complain about how depressed you are
because of the things you don't possess,
then take out your aggressions on the company
by suing them for job stress.
Your refrigerator at home is bare.
You have no bread or meat.
But the Bible tells us that he who doesn't work,
surely will not eat.

You agreed to come to work as scheduled,
but make excuses to stay away.
But when checks are scheduled to be passed out,
you're always present on that day.
You put your relatives up to calling your boss
to tell her that you're sick.

Your absence is really no big deal,
'cause when present, you don't work a lick.

The Lord was gracious to put us on the earth
for us to work the ground,
but all you want to do is sit,
that's why your butt's so round.
When other employees get their raises,
you treat them nasty and unkind.
You can get a raise yourself,
if you would first elevate your mind.

I have seen cases where people who have no medical insurance have sustained an injury outside of a job, then secured a position within a company only to tell a lie a few short weeks after being hired—that they were injured on the job—so that they can submit a disability claim and stay home while being paid. Their new employer is then responsible for paying their medical and rehabilitative expenses in addition to paying already overinflated premiums due to similar abuses to the system. When people lie and play games with the system, someone is victimized and someone must pay. That someone can be the business owner, its "valued customers" and perhaps even its employees. People can sometimes be so selfish; they are not bothered by the sufferings that they cause others unless it somehow affects them.

Everyone seems to be concerned about what their company can do for them, but few seek to make a positive impact on their company. The rate of unemployment in many areas is on a steady incline, all too often because people are unwilling to start out at the bottom. They say they can't find a job, but God tells us to seek and we will find, and that the harvest is plentiful but it is the workers that are few. Some people are too lazy or uncommitted to even seek a job with diligence. It seems that everyone wants to start out on top and be the boss, but few want to work their way up to such a position.

Eating is a gift of God, and although everyone wants to eat—and in order for us to live, we all *must* eat—few want to work for their food but would rather eat the bread of idleness. In order for us to eat, however, according to the Word of God, we *must* work (2 Thes 3:10). God merely loaned us our lives; for our lives are not our own but His. If He is gracious enough to give us the gift of eating, which sustains our life, then the very least we can do in return is to appreciate that life enough to work diligently to sustain it, because that is our lot. Ecclesiastes 2:24 says that, "A man can do nothing better than to eat and drink and *find* satisfaction in his work." Instead of finding satisfaction in our work, however, many find (or seek to find) satisfaction in the things that our work affords us—nice cars, homes, private schools and colleges for our children, name-brand clothes, etc. If we seek, instead, to find satisfaction in our work, I believe our lives will be much more meaningful and fulfilled.

Inasmuch as I am outdone by some of the rude behaviors that exist out in the business world, I am even more awestruck, surprised and thankful when I occasionally encounter someone who is extremely honest, caring and serving. These are the people who make me glad there is a "business world"; a place where I can go and enjoy the company of others with whom I feel comfortable; a place where I am known and recognized as valuable; a place where I can freely be me. Once in a while in the business world, I run into someone who actually calls me back when they said they would, or someone who wanted me to pardon their inconveniences enough to compensate me in some way; even someone who gave me more than I deserved, more than I could have even thought... just because.

There have been days when I was really going through it and God strategically placed different people from the business world in my path who have really been a blessing to my life; like the man at the Bay Bridge tollbooth who told me—not once, but twice—that he loved me and God loves me, too, and several different persons at different mail centers who have been an encouragement to me on numerous occasions when my spirits were low, and one particular person who I know in the business world, who loves me so much that she sometimes gives me things for free just because she loves me. God wants us to be honest in all of our business dealings, caring and serving—considering one another at all times. He wants us to be faithful to our word, doing what we say we will do and being true to our promises, just as He is true to His promises. He wants us to forgive others for their many shortcomings, mistakes and faults just as He forgives us—even in the business world. He also wants us to love and to give to one another, just as He loved us enough to give of His very life, for us.

A friend of mine who works as a church administrator blessed my life by sharing a prayer that he wrote and prays each morning before starting his day at work:

My Workplace Prayer

My Heavenly Father, as I enter this workplace,
I bring Your presence with me.
I speak Your peace, Your grace, Your mercy,
and Your perfect order into this office.
I acknowledge Your power over all
that will be spoken, thought, decided and done
within these walls.
Lord, I thank You for the gifts with which You
have blessed me.
I commit to using them responsibly in Your honor.
Give me a fresh supply of strength to do my job.
Anoint my projects, ideas and energy
so that even my smallest accomplishments
may bring You glory.
Lord, when I am confused, guide me.
When I am weary, energize me.
When I am burned out, infuse me with the light
of the Holy Spirit.
Keep my body healthy and strong.
May the work that I do, and the way that I do it,
bring faith, joy and a smile to all
those with whom I come into contact today.
When I leave this place, give me traveling grace
and mercy.

Bless my family and home to be in order, as it was when I left it.
I thank you for everything You have done, everything You are doing,
and everything You are going to do in my life.
May I always listen to your voice.
May I always put my faith and trust in You.
I pray that I will never do anything without consulting with You first.
Help me to always remember that nothing is about me,
but everything I do and think is about You.
In the Name of Jesus I pray,

with much love and thanksgiving. Amen.

Church Folk

And He is the head of the body, the church.
(Col 1:18a)

In this present age, a church is oftentimes referred to as a building where people gather together for worship, a place with cushioned pews, stained-glass windows and a high steeple. Although some people go to church to praise and worship God, to be strengthened by His Word and to be healed and delivered of their sins, still others attend church for superficial reasons. Some people attend church as a ritualistic celebration of a particular holiday, like Easter or Mother's Day. Some attend because they are required by their parents to attend, or because churchgoing was established early on in their lives as a routine by their parents. Still, others attend church to impress other churchgoers by their attendance. Some attend so that they can have a social outlet, show off their new clothes, select a churchgoing mate or be entertained by the choir. The Bible, on the other hand, never refers to the church as a building but as a body of Believers in Christ Jesus (Col 1:24b). We, who believe that Christ Jesus is the Son of God, and accept His free gift of salvation through the shedding of His blood, and His lordship over our lives, therefore, are the church. We understand our commission to "go" and make disciples of all nations, and therefore, understand that our real work, as Christians, exists not inside the church building but outside of it.

Oftentimes, people attend church in order to get into the presence of God. In the eyes of God, however, our bodies are the building, the temple where God's Spirit resides (1 Col 6:19), and instead of going to church to get in His presence, Believers in Christ Jesus bring the Spirit of God into the church building with them when they enter in. We do not become members of a church simply to receive from the church (having access to a pastor to perform our family members' weddings and funerals, a place where we can go to hear the Word of God, etc.), but we also become members of a church so that we can contribute to the worship experience, giving of our time, our talents and our treasures. We continue attending church Sunday after Sunday because we know that faith comes from hearing the Word of God, and because we know that living in this world requires that our faith be continuously strengthened, we must continue feeding our faith with the message, and thus, churchgoing becomes a perpetual and natural part of our spiritual lives.

We do not go to church as an expression of our holiness. We go to church so that our faith may increase, and thus, through our faith, we can be made righteous. We, who are Believers, realize that we are no better than anyone else. We just commit ourselves to the grace of God to help us to do better and to live a life that separates us from sin. We further realize that inasmuch as one man sins, we all sin because we all have a sinful nature and are capable of the filthiest of sins. If it were not for the grace of God, our lives would be led by sin, and we would be slaves to sin, just like the nonbeliever. But God stepped in and by His grace declared us righteous; not because we observe the law, but because through the law we became conscious of sin.

This righteousness that is freely given by God is given to *all* of us who believe. If we believe that we receive this righteousness that God gives us, not based on our works or the things that we do or do not do, but on our faith in the things that God does in us, through Christ, then naturally, as we become conscious of sin, we begin to walk more and more upright. As our faith begins to increase more and more, so does our consciousness toward sin, and thus, we begin to walk even more in righteousness. But even though we may walk in the righteousness that God gave us, still we know that all of our righteous acts are nothing but filthy rags; we must therefore believe that we are the righteousness of God, for we know that it is not enough for us to simply believe that God exists, but if His Spirit is really manifested in our lives, then we would begin to be more like Him, taking on more and more of His traits. We therefore attend church services regularly in order that we might get a greater understanding of who Jesus was and how He lived, so that we can follow His example, patterning our lives to be more like His.

Jesus wants us *all* to come to Him. He did not tell us to come to a church building but to come to *Him*. Because the Spirit of God does not dwell in the hearts of some of the people who enter a church building, and because we may not be well acquainted with folk enough to recognize their fruit (love, joy, peace, patience, gentleness, kindness, goodness, faithfulness, self-control), then we cannot always determine in whose heart the Spirit resides, and cannot always depend on its presence in a church building. We must, therefore, learn how to come to Jesus without having to walk into a building. Because God is a Spirit, we must worship Him in spirit and in truth. We must open our spirit to receiving His leadership and His guidance. Some church buildings, on the other hand, being full of people who are part of God's church, people who are true Believers, are overflowing with the

Spirit of God because the Believers brought the Spirit of the Lord with them into the church building, and therefore, churchgoing can be a very effective means of getting into the presence of the Lord.

Jesus wants us *all* to come to Him (whether or not we believe in Him, have fancy clothes to wear, speak in tongues, know any Scriptures or are going through some serious life challenges). His door is always open for anyone who will enter in. Satan, on the other hand, does everything he can to keep people from coming to church, trying his best to keep people away from the presence of God and His people. Many people, therefore, do not attend church because, for one reason or another, satan has convinced them that the notion of going to church is not for them.

There are a variety of different reasons/excuses that people give for not attending church services regularly. Oftentimes, folk get the righteousness thing twisted. They believe that the ones of us who go to church and believe in Jesus Christ do so as an expression of our obedience to God—because we are doing what is expected of us, as though we are claiming to be free of sin. Because they, themselves, do not feel worthy of going to church, thinking that their salvation is based on their righteousness, they not only rebel against going, but at the same time they point out everyone else's many shortcomings in an effort to prove that none of us deserve to go to church, either.

Because misery loves company, they are more able to deal with the guilt that they have toward their not deserving to attend church when they can prove that other people who attend regularly, based on their sinful behaviors and shortcomings, do not deserve to be there, either.

Oftentimes, people have their own ideas as to how we, as Christians, should behave, think and speak. They are quick to throw up in our faces the fact that they thought we were Christians when we do not behave, think and speak the way they expect us to. However, if we allow love and the peace of God to rule our every move and thought, as we treat others the way we, ourselves, would want to be treated—even when we do not want to—then we are allowing the Spirit of God to be the Lord of our lives, and not the opinions and ideology of others.

God does not separate the horrible Christians from the not-so-horrible Christians the way we do. As a matter of fact, some people who are nonbelievers exhibit more Christlike behaviors than those of us who call ourselves Christians. No matter how Christlike we try to be or claim to be, in the eyes of God all of us are dirty and all of our righteous acts have fallen short. Yet as misbehaved as we are, still He loves us all very much. If it were not for the fact that He loves us so much, all of us would be dead forever because even while we were sinners, Christ died for us, and since the wages of sin is death, Christ died in our stead so that we could all have eternal life.

Because God loves us so much, and desires that we all believe in Him, He'll take any one of us who is willing to come to Him. He'll take us with our hands trembling, eyes bucked wide, lips dry, white and quivering, hungover from an addiction. He'll take us after we've lied, cheated, stolen and dishonored. It is His desire that we all are saved.

Satan does all he can to make us think that we are undeserving of God's salvation that is given to us freely, as a gift to all who have faith to receive it. All we have to do is go to Him and let Him know that we want it, and receive it. If we do not receive it, however, we will not get it. Oftentimes, people do not believe that they deserve this free gift because of some of the awful things that they have done in their life—things for which they have not forgiven themselves. They therefore, do not believe that God will forgive them. On the contrary, God has already forgiven us all, washing away *all* of our sins, when He sent His Son to die for us. Just as He freely gives us salvation, He had to first freely forgive us for our sins. Forgiveness, therefore, is also ours for the taking. If we believe it, then we will receive it.

Oftentimes, people, not believing that the gift of salvation is free, try to purchase their own salvation. Satan uses religion to confuse us, causing us to think that if we do certain things religiously, then we will be saved; things like passing out food to the homeless every Thanksgiving, then we hope that there will be food left over so that we, ourselves, will not have to cook, attending church services regularly and sitting in the same seat every Sunday so when the pastor and everyone else looks around, they would know that we were there. Some people like to be involved in, and perhaps even the leader of, various church ministries (the choir, usher board, deacon board, etc.), and use this as a social outlet because they have no friends. While others pay tithes and offerings regularly, in hopes of being one of the top twenty tithers who are entitled to attend the annual banquet that the pastor holds, then they say the same prayers every night before going to bed and before every meal like their parents taught them when they were children, and refrain from smoking, drinking, cursing and dancing. We should not do the "religious" things we do because we are trying to pay God off for His free gift, but because we are appreciative of that gift, and because we want to show our appreciation by, in return, pleasing Him. We, who are Children of God, have a strong desire to please Him—to trust and obey Him—establishing a relationship with Him, as opposed to a religion for ourselves. We know that in order to please Him, we must have faith; faith to believe that He is our God and that His Son, Jesus, is

Lord and Savior of our lives, faith to believe that all of His promises are "yes" in Christ, and "amen" to the glory of God.

Satan, the deceiver who tries to influence us by confusing religion with salvation, does everything he can to trick people into believing that the gift of salvation is not free, and that in some way, we must earn it. Some do not even consider becoming saved because they know they fall short and could never deserve God's salvation. Others of us, who also know that we fall short and that we could never be good enough to earn God's salvation, understand that God is merciful and gracious and loves us enough to save us in spite of us. Still, some, on the other hand, actually believe that they are living good enough lives to be able to earn God's salvation. ✐

Saved?

You're too holy to wear earrings,
yet you have keloids and dark holes in your ears.
You say that wearing makeup is wrong,
but inside your purse there appears
lipstick, powder,
mascara and blush,
eyelash curlers, red nail polish
and an eyebrow brush.

Out in the world, you're seen
in your tight blue jeans,
looking like you've just stepped out
of a fashion magazine.
But when we go to see your pastor,
you strip your body of the world and its mess;
roll up your tight jeans
and put on your long, dreary dress.

You yank off your false hair,
then pull back what's left in a tight ponytail,
throw your jewelry in a bag of things
that you feel could take your soul to hell.
To this day, you won't speak to me
even though your holiness pastor even agreed
that God looks at the heart, beyond our faults,
and sees our needs.

Church folk partying in the clubs
can't say they see you
out there gettin' your groove on
like the rest of them do.
But every weekend at your house, the party's on,
and you get on with your groove.
Then when you get in the choir stand on Sunday,
you act like you can't move.

You don't just sing, you sang, girlfriend,
like an angel from heaven above;
melodies of sweetness,
joy, peace and love.
But during the week,
all you do is sing the blues;
talkin' 'bout how in every situation,
you're the one to lose.

The same tongue you use
to edify our Lord,
you use to gossip, belittle and curse others;
it's like a two-edged sword.
You judge everybody else
by the sins you think you've conquered.
Don't you know that you too
have fallen short of God's Word?

You're saved, and then you're unsaved.
It's no reason you're confused.

You might as well just give up hope,
'cause your 'ligion's gonna make you lose.
The Bible says, you shall know the truth,
and the truth shall set you free.
The truth is in the blood of Jesus Christ
that was shed for you and me.

So don't look toward yourself as your salvation
in the things you do and don't do.
Salvation is free and comes from Jesus Christ,
who paid the price for you.
God loved us enough to send His very best
to prove His love to you and me.
If you love Him, and give Him back your life,
He'll make you all you're supposed to be.

Then you won't be able to go around bragging
about the good works that you do
because you'll know that your works are not
your own,
but what He's done in you.
In order to do this, you must admit that with-
out Him,
you have no power.
And then your soul will be set free
as you wait upon that hour.

Although some may consider themselves religious
when they religiously attend church services on Sun-

day and/or special holidays, pay tithes and offerings regularly, take communion every time the church offers it, and observe other ordinances of the church, such as baptism—even singing songs boasting of the fact that they know they got religion because they've been baptized—satan, too, can be quite religious. Every time some of us do what is wrong, he religiously tries to make us feel bad about it. Every time some of us fail, he religiously tries to discourage us. And every time we open ourselves up to him, he religiously steals, kills and destroys. However, religion that God accepts as pure and faultless does not deal with the things we do in the church building but with the things we do for the church of God; looking after orphans and widows in their distress and keeping ourselves from being polluted by the world (Js 1:27). Even then, if we fail to keep a tight rein on our tongue, but instead go around boasting about all that we do for others, and all that we do to remain unpolluted, then our religion is worthless, and we only deceive ourselves into thinking that we are religious.

People who attend church regularly sometimes focus on *their* religion as opposed to their relationship with others. They speed into the church parking lot—almost hitting other churchgoing pedestrians—with their grandmother's handicapped placard on the mirror of their car so they can get the same handicapped spot that they religiously get, and run into the church to sit in the seat where they religiously sit. They religiously come to church, Sunday after Sunday, but they never *invite* anyone else. After church on Sundays, they call other church members, religiously, to criticize the pastor's sermon and to discuss the horrible sins that other members of the church are committing, so that they can feel better about the "not-so-bad" ones that they religiously commit.

Some people are quick to judge others based on the sins that they commit. But because all of us have sinned, we are *all* guilty of sin. Therefore, not one of us can point our finger at anyone else, judging others for their sins, because we are also judged by our conduct according to our own standards; standards that we have for ourselves and for others (Ezek 7:27). Because when we judge others, we get judged back in the same way and by the same measurements that we judge others; some folk who go around judging everybody else so harshly must live very secretive lives, always making sure to conceal their sins, shortcomings and fears in an attempt not to get judged back.

Unlike God, man, who looks at the outer appearance of things, has a tendency to make judgments on things that they see with their eyes. When church folk see a person crying in church—even Sunday after Sunday— they assume that the person is sad, when in actuality, they might be so full of joy that their spirit cannot contain it all. When church folk see a pregnant, unwed teen, they naturally assume that she is sad and embarrassed by her sin, encouraging her to keep her head up and instructing her to ask for God's forgiveness, when in actuality, she may have already asked God for forgiveness of her sin, accepted it and the fact that she will soon be blessed with a baby who is fearfully and wonderfully made. When church folk do not see you in church for a couple of Sundays in a row, they automatically assume that you have been staying home because you have been losing your faith, when in actuality, you might have gone out of town on vacation or for a Christian conference, and participated in worship services elsewhere. When church folk see that a person is able to quote Scripture after Scripture from the Bible, they automatically assume that the person has a close walk with the Lord, when in actuality, the person may not know the Lord at all but only remembered Scriptures because they were bored while locked in their jail cell and there was nothing else for them to read. But faith, being sure of what we hope for and certain of what we do not see, causes those of us who believe in the power of God to refrain from making premature judgments on people, situations and things, and instead, to wait on God to bring to light what is hidden in the darkness.

Sometimes we judge, categorize the severity of and compare our sins to the sins of others, as though some people, because their sins are *worse* than ours deserve everything they get. We are quick to condemn people who have chosen not to turn away from their sins, and are now suffering the consequences of those sins; consequences that they, being forewarned, "deserve."

We are quick to use phrases and Scriptures like, "What goes around, comes around," "That which you reap, you sow," "You live by the sword, you die by the sword," "Judge not, that ye be not judged," and "Every dog has his day," when it comes to the sins of everyone else. But when it comes to our sins, we want the Lord to have mercy on us. Although we believe that when punishment is inflicted on everyone else, they are getting what they deserve, when we commit the same sins, we are somehow able to justify our actions, convincing ourselves that what we are doing is not wrong. We harshly judge the sins of others, looking down on them for falling short, not realizing that if it weren't for God's grace and mercy, we could be in their shoes (or worse).

I Never Was

I never was addicted to drugs,
but I once had my heart calmed
while in a hospital bed
because I hit too much of the stuff.

I never was a liar,
but I once was denied a home that I really loved
because I got caught falsifying information
on my rental application.

I never was a thief,
but I was once let off the hook from going to juve-
nile hall
because I took something that I didn't want
or need—
just for the thrill of it.

I never was an alcoholic,
but I once almost passed out
from drinking too much,
just to change my state of mind.

I never was a cancer victim,
but I once choked down a pack of cigarettes a day,
after saying for years that I could quit
anytime I wanted to.

I never was a diabetic,
but I once downed hot tamales, candy bars and
ice cream
in the place of eating
nutritious meals.

I never was a heart attack survivor,
but I once hesitated to eat one,
let alone five, servings
of fruits and vegetables every day.

I never was committed to my grave,
but I once was dead,
but now, thank God...
I'm alive in Jesus Christ!

Because we all have sinned, and because the wages of sin is death, all of us deserve to die, to be destroyed and to self-destruct in every area of our lives. Not one of us deserves any good thing, but because of our sinfulness, we deserve all of the bad things that happen to us; those inflicted by satan, ourselves and others. None of us deserve to breathe, to prosper, to be in good health or to even have a relationship with God. Not one of us deserves God's grace (His not allowing us to get the bad things that we do deserve) nor His mercy (His giving us those blessings which we do not deserve). But God is faithful to be full of mercy and grace, and because He justifies us through the redemption that came by Christ Jesus, He prevents us from getting the things we deserve, and helps us to get the things we do not deserve.

Many people do not find it necessary to go to church and are quick to say that as a Believer, you do not have to go to church to believe in God or to be saved. They further say that they can stay home and read their Bible, pray, fellowship with Believers outside of the church and get the Word from television and radio. After all, faith does come from hearing the Word of God, and you don't have to go to church to hear the Word these days. I, myself, would have to agree that it is a blessing to be able to receive the message of the Gospel through such convenient means as television, radio and even the Internet. We are so blessed in America to have such strong access to hearing the Gospel of Jesus Christ. Some people, including myself, have even become addicted to watching one televangelist after another, and are oftentimes considered televangeholics. As a matter of fact, when I heard about Christian television channels, I started receiving satellite television services, just so I could partake in this tremendous opportunity to continuously feed my spirit with the Word of God by way of television in the comfort of my own home. ❧

Disturbing the Peace

One night, I was at home alone,
minding business of my own,
when I got a visit from the police.
He said the neighbors had been complaining
about the noisy folk we were entertaining,
and declared that we were disturbing the peace.
They figured there was a party going on,
but for some strange reason,
the cars were all gone,
that belonged to the people inside.

They assumed, because of all the noise we were
making,
that we must have been drinking
and probably taking drugs
because the noise was undignified.
I softly said, "Sir, what are you talking about?
I'm home all by myself,
and here without any type of company.
Won't you come on in?"
As he stepped inside and looked around,
I could see he looked confused,
wondering where all my company went,
and where was all the booze?
He could find no evidence inside my home
of any type of sin.

"As you can see with your very own eyes,
it's just me, the Good Lord and my big-screen TV
Won't you have a seat?"
He said he had been sitting down all day
and felt more comfortable earning his pay
by standing on his feet.
Then he asked me if I would kindly turn the TV
down
because it was up so loud that it almost drowned
me out,
and he could barely hear me
say what I had to say,
so I kindly obliged.
There was a sweet peace that filled the inside.

He didn't understand why all my neighbors
would complain about me that way,
and pondered over what it was that they had heard;
kept badgering me about the nature of the noise,
but I assured him that I was home all by myself.
He asked me what I was doing while home alone
because the reasons for the complaints,
to him, were unknown.
I turned the TV back up and told him,
"You can see for yourself."
I admitted to him that when I watch TV,
I sometimes get out of hand.
Then I asked him one more time to sit,
but he said he'd rather stand.

Although his standing made me uncomfortable,
he said he'd be just fine.
I warned him that I sometimes lose control
when I watch my TV screen,
and although I may appear meek and mild,
I often shout and scream.
I further admitted that I get influenced
by some special friends of mine:
You see, there's Creflo Dollar,
who makes me holler,
and Joyce Meyer,
who sets my soul on fire.
Then there's Joel Osteen,
who makes me scream,
and Bishop Jakes,
who always makes
me forget where I am.
Eddie Long has me up in here singing my song,
and Paula White takes me to higher heights.
Noel Jones is like fire caught up in my bones.
My good friends John Hagee,
Zachary, Juanita and Angie Ray
all make me want to stay
at home and get my praise on.
So, if we are disturbing the peace
by celebrating God's Holy Word,
then go ahead and lock me up
and throw away the key.

*Just make sure that my jail cell is equipped
with a satellite and a big-screen TV.*

Inasmuch as I love watching some of these great
women and men of God on television, attending their
conferences and seminars, and listening to good
preaching and gospel singing on the radio, I, too, very
much enjoy attending church services on Sundays,
fellowshipping with other Believers with whom I am
familiar and with those who are eager to do the same;
eager to wake up on Sunday mornings, determined
to make the day holy, eager to be in the presence of
the Almighty God, and eager to praise and worship
God in the midst of people who, too, love to praise and
worship Him. Although church membership or even
regular church attendance are not prerequisites for
salvation, still, why would a Believer *not* want to be
in the midst of other Believers to attain the same
goal—worshipping their Savior and Lord?

The Bible says that, as Believers, we are not to forsake the assembling of ourselves together with other
Believers (Heb 10:25 KJV). People who like to watch
football games like to be around other people who like
to watch football games so they can talk about and
enjoy football games together. People who like to talk
politics like to be around other people who like to
talk politics. People who like to keep up with the latest fashions like to talk to other people who like to

keep up with the latest fashions. So, it is only natural that people who love to praise, worship and grow in the Lord want to be around other people with whom they have things in common.

Some people stay away from church because they have issues with some pastors in the churches. They believe that many pastors are crooks, swindling church members out of their money so that they can drive around in expensive cars and live lavish lifestyles. They also believe that many pastors are the biggest sinners of all because they lie, cheat and steal. Unfortunately, in many instances, these beliefs are true, and in many cases, some pastors fail to preach about those sins of which they themselves are guilty of committing, for fear of having to look at their own sins. Oftentimes, because of these different stigmas that are placed upon pastors, some of them, not wanting to look money hungry, water down teachings about the importance of paying tithes and offerings or, in order to avoid being accused of improper behavior, fail to greet their members with holy kisses as the Spirit urges them to do, or because their every move is being judged, fear being the bold men and women of God that they were called to be.

Pastors, like the rest of us, although expected to live clean and moral lives, too, fall short. Like the rest of us, there is no excuse for their falling short, but because they are nothing more than human beings, existing out of the same sinful flesh as the rest of us, they, too, miss the mark of perfection. We, therefore, must never look toward any pastor (or any person, for that matter) as the one whom we are to emulate, but to Jesus Christ, the only perfect person who has ever walked the earth. Just like the rest of us, pastors excel in some areas but are weak in others.

Some people refuse to go to church because of all the problems and chaos going on in the church caused by hatred, gossip, jealousy, cliques, judgments, division and dissension—especially amongst the sisters in the church. Galatians 5:15 says that if we keep on biting and devouring each other, we had better watch out or we will be destroyed by one another. One would think that because these sisters show up to church services week after week, that the Word they hear would penetrate their hearts and cause them to take a good look at themselves and see where they fall short. But, either they do not go to church to become more like God and instead, focus on everyone else's shortcomings, or the Word in which they hear does not address their evil ways, or they honestly do not know what they are doing to others, and they need someone to specifically point out their area of weakness.

Well, here goes:

Sisters, Can We All Just Get Along?

To My Dear Sisters in Christ:

Wouldn't it be nice
if we could just get along
and come together in peace and harmony?
Instead, we cause division because all we think
about is
"I," "myself" and "me."

We can't stand to have each other in our homes,
or so it seems to me.
It's as though everybody's afraid of being judged
by what the others may see.
When we do have sisters come to our homes,
our men are hid off in our bedrooms
for fear that it may ruin our chances
for a wedding and a honeymoon.

We search for reasons to dislike one another
so we can toss each other out
of our lives before it's found out
what we're really all about.
We trick others into thinking
that they can confide in us,
then as soon as someone lets us down,
that's when we betray her trust.

We click, we gossip, we cast others out
until they feel insecure,
then walk around with our heads held high,
pretending our love is pure.
We go around telling all our friends about
how some sister did us wrong
just because she was obedient,
when asked to lead our song.

We tell sisters to come as they are;
don't let an opportunity pass you by,
then judge them on the clothes they wear
because their fashions are so fly.
We wear big hats and sit on the front row,
blocking everyone else's view,
then get mad when the usher comes over
and motions for us to move.

We get up on the usher board, looking mean
and refusing to smile and speak.
That's why the church has a bad reputation
and its attendance is so weak.
When asked how we're doing, we say we're
blessed;
acting like our faith is strong.
Sisters, my sisters, can we stop the madness,
and all just get along?

Inasmuch as people can come up with excuse after excuse for staying away from church, many people do not even understand why they are coming up with excuses to prevent them from attending. Many do not realize that satan, the evil devil, is doing all he can to keep negativity, chaos and confusion stirring inside and outside of the church building and the Church Body so that people will stay away and not hear about the salvation that comes from God through Jesus Christ. Satan hates it when we come together as one to glorify, praise and worship our Father. Although it is God's desire that we all become His Children and follow Him, satan, being a stumbling block, wants us to give up on this whole notion of receiving God's salvation, and follow his desires so that he, the father of lies, can be our father. He wants to keep us trapped in sin and unrighteousness and prevent us from loving our brothers so that we cannot become Children of God. He does everything he can to keep our minds busy, involved and consumed with things of this world, like pleasing and hating others, expanding our careers, keeping up with the Joneses, keeping our minds fuzzy from drugs and hungover from alcohol, low self-esteem, defeat, sporting activities, stresses, inadequate rest, selfish, envious, resentful and vengeful thoughts and ideas, etc., in hopes that by the time Sunday comes around, we won't even think about going to church, let alone salvation of our souls.

Once we become Children of God, we become an even bigger threat to satan because we are now empowered and equipped to help to bring others into the army of God (perhaps hundreds, thousands and even millions). When God's children become Children of God, we oftentimes operate under the misconception that our lives will be without spiritual conflict and thus, when we are faced with battles—finances, divorce, death of a loved one, rejection, wrongdoings, failures, sickness and disease, dealing with our children who are lost in sin, etc.—if God does not come to our rescue when, where and how we expect Him to, we automatically think that He is not on our side, and we turn away from Him and become our own god, doing our own thing.

Because we are Children of God, satan desires to attack us with all kinds of sins so that we will lose hope in the God of our salvation and prevent others from joining God's army. He uses all kinds of manipulative schemes to try and cause us to forget about God's goodness so that we can feel defeated; like victims, and not victors. There is a spiritual battle going on between God and the enemy. Prior to our becoming Children of God, they were both battling for our souls to determine where we would spend eternity; heaven or hell. Then, once we became Children of God, they began battling for our spirits to determine how we would spend our lives here on earth; whether prosperous, victorious and abundant, or not. This battle, unlike others, is not a physical one like the ones we have read about in the New Testament of the Bible, the wars and rumors of wars about which we have been warned in the Old Testament, or even the ones we continue to read about in newspapers and watch on television today. This battle of which I am speaking is not a fight for our flesh and blood but a fight for our souls and our spirits. This battle is not against nations and powers on this earth, but against the rulers, authorities and powers of this dark world and against the spiritual forces of evil in the heavenly realms. This battle is a fight between good and evil— God and the devil.

Although this battle is being played out in the hearts and history of mankind, God has promised us that one day He will be victorious over satan through His Son, Christ Jesus; that He would soon crush satan under the feet of the Believers. As Believers, we must believe that the God of our fathers, who is mighty in power, will rule over all the kingdoms of the nations, and that all power and might are in His hand, and that no one can withstand Him. We must proclaim the power of God, whose majesty is over Israel, and whose power is in the skies. We must believe that even though satan may kill, steal and destroy some of us, one day the Lord is going to get him, once and for all.

Get Him, Lord

Every time I try to love,
somebody lets me down.
Every time I step out to give,
disappointment always abounds.
Satan is out there doing his thing,
trying to make a beast of me.
Sometimes all I want is to be alone,
away from society.
Then I realize I have no friends,
as I sit around lonely and bored.
I don't want to have to live like this,
so get him, Lord... Get him, Lord.

My finances sometimes get out of whack
to the point of no return.
My debts are often bigger
than the paycheck that I earn.
When bill collectors call my home,
I'm tempted to change my voice.
I hate to have to lie like that,
so I make the righteous choice.
Satan tries to convince me
that the very air I breathe,
I can't afford.
I'm trying to buy myself some time
while You get him, Lord... Get him, Lord.

Living righteously and holy
is sometimes hard to do.
It's like temptations to sin are everywhere,
and always stalking you.
Sometimes I want to throw in the towel
and say, "Forget this mess,
let me just live my life for myself,
and act like all the rest."
Then I think about Your goodness,
and how Your love for me was poured.
I'm just going to stand and wait
while You get him Lord... Get him, Lord.

This battle never was mine to fight;
it's always been Yours, anyway.
So I surrender all I have,
and I'm giving it to You today.
Satan thinks he has it going on,
but he's a defeated foe.
When he gets up in my face,
I'll tell him where to go.
And when this world is over,
I'll get my just reward,
because in the end,
I know that You are going to
get him, Lord.

Although Children of God were already chosen by
Him, still, we, ourselves, must make the decision to

serve Him and to take our stand against the evil one. We must decide against whom we are fighting; whether we are Children of God, and are against the enemy, or whether we are children of satan, the devil, and are against God. If we do not make a decision, then satan, the prince of this world, will automatically claim us as his, by default.

Before we, soldiers of God's army, go into battle, we must first ask God for wisdom, which is supreme and better than weapons of war. We must be wise, and not foolish, so that we may understand what the Lord's will is for our lives; whether or not we should go forth, stop or wait, to whom we should go, stop or wait, where we should go, stop or wait, when we should go, stop or wait, and why we should go, stop or wait. Then we must ask God for our weapons that are necessary to equip us for battle so that we can defeat satan's cause, the very reason that Jesus, Himself, appeared. If we believe we will be given wisdom and weapons needed for our battles, then we will receive them.

Although we live in the world, however, we do not wage war as the world does. Therefore, the weapons with which we fight are not the weapons of the world—bombs, guns or weapons of mass destruction. On the contrary, they have divine power to demolish disguised traps set up for us by the enemy. We must, therefore, demolish arguments and every pretension that sets itself up against the knowledge of God, take captive every thought to make it obedient to Christ and be ready to punish every act of disobedience, once our obedience is complete. Because satan is the prince of this world, those of us who are Children of God begin to feel more and more like aliens and strangers in this world the closer we walk with the Father, and we therefore begin to abstain from our sinful desires, which war against our soul. •

Prior to going into battle, we must make sure that we are properly prepared for battle so that we can firmly take our stand against the devil's schemes. We must, therefore, put on the full armor of God; the belt of *truth* (Jn 14:6) buckled around our waist, the breastplate of *righteousness* in place, our feet fitted with readiness that comes from the gospel of *peace,* the shield of *faith* taken up so that we can extinguish all the flaming arrows of the evil one, the helmet of *salvation* and the sword of the Spirit (the Word of God). We must remain self-controlled and alert, always on the lookout for the enemy, who prowls around like a roaring lion, looking for someone to devour, knowing that if we resist him, not giving him a foothold, but standing firm in the faith, submitting ourselves to God—as it is He who drives out fear—then the evil devil will flee from us.

In this battle, as Children of God, we must fight! If we do not, the devil will stomp us to death with sin. We must, therefore, be spiritually strong, and fight the Lord's battles as He fights our battles for us. We must not go into battle fearing satan, for God did not give us a spirit of fear, but of power, and of love, and of a sound mind. As we fight, we must not fight like a wimp beating the air, but by putting up our dukes and beating off the devilish schemes of satan, refusing to lie down and play dead. We must trust in God for our victory, realizing that the battle does not belong to us, but Him. If we trust in God, we have no reason to fear satan, as he wants us to, but we will believe that, through the Word of God, we have been given the authority to trample on snakes and scorpions and to overcome all the power of the enemy, and that nothing will harm us because we are more than conquerors through the love of God. We further believe that no weapon formed against us will prevail because the Lord is our defense, and that through the joy of Christ who strengthens us, we, being victorious, can do all things.

The evil devil, the enemy of the Children of God, is trying to take as many of us captive as he possibly can, and is using various schemes against us to do so. Prior to our accepting Jesus as our Lord and Savior, the devil did all he could to try to stop us from receiving God's salvation through Christ Jesus. As Children of God, he does all he can to try to prevent us from living the victorious life that God has promised us, in hopes that we will feel too defeated to help to bring others into the knowledge of Jesus Christ. The greater our potential for bringing others into the saving knowledge of Jesus Christ, the greater of a threat we are to satan. The greater of a threat that we are to satan, the more frequent and intense will be our battles. We must, therefore, fight the good fight of faith and hold on to our confession of that faith when we accepted Jesus as our Lord and Savior.

This satan is no little red devil who runs around with a pitchfork, poking at people's bodies, but a demonic, unclean spirit that sows evil by tempting and deceiving the hearts and minds of people—both Christians and non-Christians. Because God's greatest commandments are for us to love Him with all our heart, our mind and our soul, and to love our neighbor as ourselves, satan does all he can to prevent us from doing so (and even tries to influence us to love him and to believe that he loves us) because he knows that in order for him to have our souls, he must first infiltrate our mind and our heart. Because the Lord searches the heart and examines the mind to reward a man according to his conduct, according to what his deeds deserve, satan wants to darken our understanding and separate us from the life of God by influencing us to be ignorant due to the hardening of our hearts so that we will lose all sensitivity and give ourselves over to sensuality and indulge in every kind of impurity, with a continual lust for more, so that we will not be rewarded but punished.

Satan is fully aware of the fact that out of the heart come evil thoughts—murder, adultery, sexual immorality, theft, false testimony and slander—things that make man unclean, like him. He further understands that if he can enter the minds of people and prevent them from thinking it worthwhile to retain the knowledge of God, they can be given a depraved mind, to do what ought not to be done. It is then that their hearts and minds can become filled with every kind of wickedness, evil, greed and depravity, full of envy, murder, strife, deceit and malice, and thus become gossips, slanderers, God-haters, insolent, arrogant and boastful, inventing ways of doing evil, disobedient to their parents, senseless, faithless, heartless, ruthless. Although they know God's righteous decree that those who do such things deserve death, they not only continue to do these very things but also approve of those who practice them.

Both satan and God want our hearts. While satan desires for us to hate God and one another, God wants us to love, obey, serve, follow and seek Him with our whole heart. God, who searches hearts and minds— our innermost being; our courage, motivations, thoughts, emotions and actions—desires that we, above all else, guard our heart, for it is the wellspring of life. He wants us to store up good things (His Word, knowledge, wisdom) in our hearts so that our words and actions will be good; for the good man brings good things out of the good stored up in his heart (Lk 6:45) and out of the overflow of the heart, the mouth speaks (Mt 12:34).

Similarly, both satan and God desire to have our minds, which is the battlefield. Satan, knowing that the mind of sinful man is death, but the mind controlled by the Spirit of God is life and peace, prepares his deadly weapons, making ready his flaming arrows. His desire is that our minds remain on earthly, unspiritual and sinful things, being hostile to God, puffed up and corrupted by our deceitful desires. God, on the other hand, desires that our minds are made new—righteous and holy, willing, steadfast, spiritual, full of His laws, clear and self-controlled.

Inasmuch as God desires for us to renew our minds, putting off our old, sinful nature, and looking, acting and thinking more like Him, in this world where satan is prince and his followers are many, this can be quite difficult, for temptation to sin is ever present. That is why, as Children of God, although we are supposed to love everyone—even our enemies, doing good to them, blessing them and praying for them—we must not yoke ourselves together with unbelievers, but come out from amongst them and be separate; not giving over to them the things that are considered to be sacred—our families, friends, marriages, possessions and money for which we have worked hard and are near and dear to our hearts; our personal business, life's decisions, and yes, even our churches—or else, they may trample over them and tear us to pieces. If we do not separate our own selves from the wicked in this present age, we may begin to look and act like them. Then, when the angels go to doing the separating of the wicked from the righteous at the end of the age, we might look and act so much like the wicked, they may consider us to be one of them.

We, as Children of God, must, therefore, live righteous and holy, being in one heart and mind, detesting the dishonest just as the wicked detest us and caring about justice for the poor, as we deliver others from death. When we choose to live righteously, we are rewarded for doing so. We will be rescued from trouble, enjoy the fruit of our righteous deeds, be blessed and repaid at the Resurrection. Our children will also be blessed and the kingdom of heaven will belong to us. The wicked, on the other hand, being brought down by their own wickedness and trapped by their evil desires, inherit the troubles of the righteous. When the righteous prosper, the city rejoices, but when the wicked perish, there are shouts of joy and his hope perishes; all he expected from his power comes to nothing.

God wants us to be strong and courageous in fighting our battles. He wants to help us, but He expects us to ask Him for His help in acknowledgment of the fact that He is our help and our strength. God wants us to have the desires of our hearts, and He told us that if we delight ourselves in Him, He will give them to us. He wants us to come boldly to His throne of grace and ask for anything in His Son Jesus' name, so that we will receive it and our joy will be complete. He does not desire that we suffer in any way, shape or form, but that we should always prosper and be in good health, even as our souls prosper. He also wants us to love one another enough to want the same for each other.

Therefore, when we go to God in prayer, we must pray, not only for ourselves, but for one another, just as Jesus did when He showed us how we should pray. He, being the only begotten Son of God and the image of the invisible God, He, who, while we were still sinners, came to die for us, yet speaks to the Father in our defense when we sin; He, who is God, our Father, from whom all things came and for whom we live, and the Lord, Jesus Christ, through whom all things came and through whom we live; He, who could have selfishly prayed for Himself, but, instead, loved us all enough to pray for us all. If we, as Children of God, love Him, who first loved us, and without whose love we would not be able to love, then we, who have been made by Him to be a kingdom and priests to serve Him, will love one another the way that God loves us, in spite of our sins, differences and downfalls. If we truly love one another, we would be kind to one another, and not envy one another, be boastful, prideful, rude, self-seeking or easily angered. We would keep no record of wrongs or delight in evil, but would rejoice with the truth. Just as God continues to bear with us, believe in us, hope in us and endure in us, we must always bear with, and believe, hope and endure in one another, in hopes that somebody will come correct, as we ourselves are coming correct and as our God, who is, was and is to come...correct.

Dr. Jacqueline Lawrence recently relocated to Dallas, Texas, where she is enjoying her career as an author.

Message From The Author

To My Dear Brothers and Sisters
(In Christ, I Pray):

I haven't always been as good, loving, patient, kind, joyous, gentle, self-controlled, faithful and peaceful as I should have been, with you. Please forgive me, each and every one of you, *as I forgive you*, for any negative thought that I have ever thought about you, word that I have ever spoken against you and unrighteous act that I have ever done to you. Forgive me also, *as I forgive you,* for the times when I have been a stumbling block, and kept you from getting closer to God with the sins that I have committed and omitted. Like me, you, too, are our Father's child, His precious lamb. He loves you like He loves me. He died for you, like He died for me. Because we are all His children, we are brothers and sisters with the same Father, the same friend, the same husband, the same Lord. Because I love Him and He loves you, I must love you, too.

I pray that you, too, would rid yourself of all your offenses and love your brothers and sisters—even your enemies—so that our Father's light will shine through us, and so we can draw others toward Him, through us. Let's love!

In Jesus' name,
Dr. Jacqueline Lawrence